First World War
and Army of Occupation
War Diary
France, Belgium and Germany

16 DIVISION
47 Infantry Brigade
Leicestershire Regiment
14th Battalion
1 August 1918 - 30 April 1919

WO95/1970/5

The Naval & Military Press Ltd
www.nmarchive.com
Published in association with The National Archives

Published by

The Naval & Military Press Ltd

Unit 10 Ridgewood Industrial Park,

Uckfield, East Sussex,

TN22 5QE England

Tel: +44 (0) 1825 749494

www.naval-military-press.com

www.nmarchive.com

This diary has been reprinted in facsimile from the original. Any imperfections are inevitably reproduced and the quality may fall short of modern type and cartographic standards.

© Crown Copyright
Images reproduced by permission of The National Archives, London, England, 2015.

Contents

Document type	Place/Title	Date From	Date To
Heading	WO95/1790 16 Div-47 Inf Bde 14 Leicestershire Regt Aug 1918-Apr 1919		
Heading	16th Division 47th Infy Bde 14th Bn Leicester Regt Aug 1918-Apl 1919 Forward With June 1918 observing 2/4 Battalion To From 30.7.18		
War Diary	Doudeauville (13. Calais 5 D 9.4)	01/08/1918	11/08/1918
War Diary	Enguinhalt R 33 B 7.2 36 E 1/40,000	11/08/1918	19/08/1918
War Diary	Noeux-Les Mines 44 B 1/40000 K 24 A 5.5.	20/08/1918	21/08/1918
War Diary	G2d 0.0. Gorre. Map. 1/20000	22/08/1918	31/08/1918
Operation(al) Order(s)	14th, Leicestershire Regiment. Battalion Order No. 1. 11.8.18	11/08/1918	11/08/1918
Operation(al) Order(s)	14th, Leicestershire Regt. Order No. 2. 18th, August 1918.	18/08/1918	18/08/1918
Operation(al) Order(s)	14th, Leicestershire Regiment Order No. 3	20/08/1918	20/08/1918
Operation(al) Order(s)	14th, Leicestershire Regiment Order No. 4.	30/08/1918	30/08/1918
War Diary	Noeux-Les-Mines. K 24 a. 5.5.	01/09/1918	06/09/1918
War Diary	Annequin F 29 C 62.	07/09/1918	08/09/1918
War Diary	Sheet 44 A. G 2 C 81.	09/09/1918	09/09/1918
War Diary	Sheet 44 A 1/40,000 Gorre Sheet 1/20000 G2 C 81	10/09/1918	12/09/1918
War Diary	Annequin Sheet 44 B 1/40000	13/09/1918	13/09/1918
War Diary	Gorre Sheet. G 2 C 8.1	14/09/1918	20/09/1918
War Diary	G2c 8.1.	21/09/1918	22/09/1918
War Diary	Lozinghem C 18 C. Sheet 44 B 1/40000	23/09/1918	30/09/1918
Operation(al) Order(s)	14th Bn. Leicestershire Regiment Order No. 5.		
Operation(al) Order(s)	14th Leicestershire Regiment Order No. 6	07/09/1918	07/09/1918
Operation(al) Order(s)	14th Leicestershire Regiment Order No. 7	11/09/1918	11/09/1918
Operation(al) Order(s)	14th Leicestershire Regiment Order No. 8	13/09/1918	13/09/1918
Operation(al) Order(s)	14th Leicestershire Regiment Order No. 9	15/09/1918	15/09/1918
Operation(al) Order(s)	14th Leicestershire Regiment Order No. 10	18/09/1918	18/09/1918
Operation(al) Order(s)	14th Leicestershire Regiment Order No. 11	20/09/1918	20/09/1918
Operation(al) Order(s)	14th Leicestershire Regiment Order No. 12	22/09/1918	22/09/1918
War Diary	Hazebrouck 5A. F6. a5.20. lozinghem.	01/10/1918	01/10/1918
War Diary	Noeux-Les-Mines	02/10/1918	02/10/1918
War Diary	44 B.K. 18. 1/40000	03/10/1918	08/10/1918
War Diary	Cambrin. 44 A O/40000 A 20	09/10/1918	09/10/1918
War Diary	Billy B 22 d.	10/10/1918	13/10/1918
War Diary	Cambrin A 20 C.	14/10/1918	15/10/1918
War Diary	Billy B 22 d.	16/10/1918	16/10/1918
War Diary	Provin C 27 A C.	17/10/1918	17/10/1918
War Diary	D 23 Sheet 44 A 1/40000 Phalempin	18/10/1918	18/10/1918
War Diary	F 21 C 17 Sheet 44 A 1/40000	19/10/1918	19/10/1918
War Diary	La. Posterie Sheet 44 1/40000 A 6 C.	20/10/1918	20/10/1918
War Diary	Rumes T 28 69.5 Sheet 37 1/40000.	21/10/1918	21/10/1918
War Diary	Taintignies U 725 d 6.2 Sheet 37 1/40000	22/10/1918	22/10/1918
War Diary	U 21 d 62. Sheet 37 1/40000	23/10/1918	24/10/1918
War Diary	Taintignies U 25 d 62	25/10/1918	25/10/1918
War Diary	Bachy T 25 C. 2.3.	26/10/1918	28/10/1918
War Diary	Bachy Sheet 37 1/40000 T 25 C.	29/10/1918	31/10/1918
Operation(al) Order(s)	14th Leicestershire Regiment Order No. 13.4.10.18	04/10/1918	04/10/1918
Miscellaneous	Daily Orders Part II.		

Type	Description	Date From	Date To
Operation(al) Order(s)	14th Leicestershire Regiment Order No. 14 7.10.18	07/10/1918	07/10/1918
Miscellaneous	Field State.		
Operation(al) Order(s)	14th Bn. Leicestershire Regt. Operation Order No. 1. 15.10.18.	15/10/1918	15/10/1918
Operation(al) Order(s)	14th Leicestershire Operation Order No. 2	15/10/1918	15/10/1918
Operation(al) Order(s)	14th Leicesters Operation Order No 4.		
Operation(al) Order(s)	14th Leicestershire Regt. Operation Order No 6	16/10/1918	16/10/1918
Operation(al) Order(s)	14th Leicestershire Regt Operation Order No 7.	17/10/1918	17/10/1918
Operation(al) Order(s)	14th Leicesters Regt. Operation Order No 8.		
Operation(al) Order(s)	14th Bn. Leicestershire Regt. Operation Order No 10.	18/10/1918	18/10/1918
Operation(al) Order(s)	14th Leicesters Regt. Operation Order No. 11		
Operation(al) Order(s)	14th Leicestershire Regt. Operation Order No 17.	21/10/1918	21/10/1918
Operation(al) Order(s)	14th Leicester Regt. Operation Order No. 19	21/10/1918	21/10/1918
Operation(al) Order(s)	14th Leicester Regt. Operation Order No. 21	22/10/1918	22/10/1918
Operation(al) Order(s)	14th Leicester Regt Operation Order No 22	23/10/1918	23/10/1918
Operation(al) Order(s)	14th Leicester Regt Order No 23	23/10/1918	23/10/1918
Operation(al) Order(s)	14th Leicestershire Regt. Operation Order No 24	24/10/1918	24/10/1918
Operation(al) Order(s)	14th Leicester Regt Order No. 25	24/10/1918	24/10/1918
Operation(al) Order(s)	14th Leicestershire Regt No 26.	25/10/1918	25/10/1918
War Diary	Sheet 37 1/40000. Bachy. T 25 C 2.3.	01/11/1918	03/11/1918
War Diary	Ennevelin. Sheet 44 A. 1/40000 F.2 B 3.2.	04/11/1918	08/11/1918
War Diary	Fretin Sheet 36 1/40000 F 21 B.8.0.	09/11/1918	10/11/1918
War Diary	El Bail Sheet 44 1/40000 Central	11/11/1918	15/11/1918
War Diary	Genech. Sheet 44 1/40000	16/11/1918	16/11/1918
War Diary	Tourmignies Sheet 44 A 1/40000 E 28 d 5.2	17/11/1918	31/12/1918
War Diary	Tourmignies	01/01/1919	31/01/1919
War Diary	Tourmignies Sheet 44 A. 1/40000	01/02/1919	30/04/1919
Map			
Map	Map B		
Miscellaneous			
Map	36th Div. Second Army Barrage Map. June. 1917		

WO95/1790

16 Div – 47 Inf Bde

14 Leicestershire Regt

Aug 1918 – Apr 1919

16TH DIVISION
47TH INFY BDE

14TH BN LEICESTER REGT
AUG 1918 - APL 1919

Formed en UK June 1918 absorbing
2/4 Battalion   To France 30.7.18

SECRET

Army Form C. 2118.

WAR DIARY
or
INTELLIGENCE SUMMARY. 14th LEICESTERS

(Erase heading not required.)

Place	Date	Hour	Summary of Events and Information	Remarks and references to Appendices
DOULIEAUVILLE (13.CALAIS 5D 9.4)	August 1918 1	9am-1pm	Training	1400
do	2	9am-	Training	1400
do	3	9am-12.30pm	Inservice Training. Musketry Training	1400
do	4	10.60 am	Battn Church Parade	1400
	5	9am-11am	Training. Company B & H & H Misses worked on 600 range	1400
			Lewis Ypres - 20/8/18	
	6	6am-2pm	Battn Training on ground. M Leh M16 & shot 300 firing	1400
	7	9am-4pm	Inservice Training	1400
	8	9am-12.30pm	2 Coys Bathing morning, 1 afternoon. 2 Coys on 600 Range morning	1400
		2pm-5pm	sport and afternoon	
	9	8am	Battn paraded ready to proceed to Training Area on R.O.L. + R27 Plof	1400
			36 E.1/40000). Training 10am - 1pm	
	10	9am-12noon	Interior Economy. Warning order received 7.30pm for Battn to	1400
			be ready to move 2 hr notice to 4th Army area 2nd Lieut T. SMITH
			2 LT G.W. SMITH joined for duty from K.I.B.D. CALAIS
	11	10 pm	Battn moved by march route to THUBEAUVILLE + ENGDIN HAUT.	1400

COMMANDING 14th Bn LEICESTERSHIRE REGT.
LIEUT.-COL.

SECRET					Army Form C. 2118.

WAR DIARY
or
INTELLIGENCE SUMMARY

14 LEICESTER REGT.

(Erase heading not required.)

Place	Date	Hour	Summary of Events and Information	Remarks and references to Appendices
ENGUINEGAT R33 B7.2	August 1918 11.	6pm	Battn HQ established at R33 B7.2. Lt Col J.C. BAINES D.S.O. reported to assume command.	Appx
36E/40000 do	12.	9-12.30 pm	C. & D Coys Bathing at DOUDEAUVILLE. A & B Coys Firing on 300yd range. Lt Col Sir I. COLQUHOUN	Appx
		2pm-5pm	A & B Coys Bathing. C & D Coys Firing on 300yd range. Lt Col Sir I. COLQUHOUN Bt DSO proceeded to take command 13th Bn Royal Scots.	
do	13.	8.30am-1pm	Battn HQ athletic & Transports to Bathing at DOUDEAUVILLE. Lt Col J.C. BAINES D.S.O. assumes command.	Appx
		9am-1pm	Individual Training.	
		6.10pm	B.O.R. found from Base	
do	14.	9am-12.30pm	Boy Training in open order attack.	Appx
do	15.	9am-12.30pm	Individual Training. Lectures by Lt Col R.B. CAMPBELL DSO	Appx
do	16.	9am-12.30pm	Individual Training. Conference at Bde HQ 10.8-10.45am	Appx
do			C.O. attended Training demonstration at HESDIGNEUL.	
do	17.	9am-1pm	Company Training. C.O. Lecture to Training 10am-12noon	Appx
			Lt. W.L. TEW. Lt. R.S. HEYWOOD 2 Lt E.A. ANGRAVE proceeded on course.	
			Received orders that Bde would move to BETHUNE AREA on 19th.	

[signature]
LIEUT.-COL.
COMMANDING 14th [BN LEICESTER REGT]

SECRET.

Army Form C. 2118.

Instructions regarding War Diaries and Intelligence Summaries are contained in F. S. Regs., Part II. and the Staff Manual respectively. Title pages will be prepared in manuscript.

WAR DIARY
or
INTELLIGENCE SUMMARY.

(Erase heading not required.)

1A LEICESTER REGT

Place	Date	Hour	Summary of Events and Information	Remarks and references to Appendices
	Aug 1918			
ENGUINHALT	18	9.45 am	Church Parade on Football Ground. C.O. + Boy Commanders went by train	
R33 B 7.2			Bus to recreation hut in HOHENZOLLERN SECTION	
36.E/1/40,000	19	5.50 am	Battn paraded at B.H.Q. & marched to HODICQ to embus 7.30 am.	
do			Embused & proceeded to NOEUX-LES-MINES arriving 3.30 p.m. Good journey. Men bivouac for night. B.H.Q. established in Quarry K24A76.5.	
NOEUX-LES-MINES 44A/1/40,000	20	9 am	Long busy for organization — intense heavy. 12 noon Advance party proceeds ahead to line. Received orders to relieve 1st Gloucesters in HOHENZOLLERN SECTION Right Bde Sector.	
K24 A 6.5				
do	21	9 am	Battn paraded & proceeded by march route to line. Very hot day. B.H.Q. established at G2d.0.0 sheet GORRE/20000 Relief completed by 4.55 pm.	
G2 d 0.0	22		In line. Quiet day. VERMELLES Shelled 6 am & 10 pm. Boys sent out	
GORRE MAP 1/20000			Liaison patrols. 2 casualties at our reception camp caused by shell. B.O. shell. Brigadier Genl went round line with L.O.	

[signature] LIEUT.-COL.
COMMANDING 14th Bn. LEICESTERSHIRE REGT.

SECRET
Army Form C. 2118.

WAR DIARY
or
INTELLIGENCE SUMMARY.
(Erase heading not required.)

14 LEICESTERS

Place	Date 1918	Hour	Summary of Events and Information	Remarks and references to Appendices
G.2.D.0.0	Aug 23		Quiet day. 2/Lt BLACKTON took out patrol from G.4.D.57.65. Australians into enemy lines to GROSS TR. G.4.B.9.1. Proceeded to G.4.B.9.3 when held up	A.G.O
GORRE MAP 1/20,000			by enemy m.m.g. returned 3 a.m.	
do	24		Quiet day. Enemy shelled SURREY & HARLEY slightly. Hostile patrol approached 1-A.28 our LEFT FRONT POSTS about 2 a.m. Driven off by rifle fire	1-A.28
do	25		Quiet day. Posts L.10 & L.9.a. shelled slightly by 4.2" H.E. Worked on improving post L.10 during night.	shell
do	26		Quiet day. Work continued on L.10 & L.16 posts during night. Enemy shelled Reserve line heavily about 2am - 2.10am. One casualty wounded. Man of wounds later at A.D.S.	A.6.Q
do	28		Fairly quiet day. CAPT WILD R. WEST KENTS proceeded to from 6th LONDONS is 2nd in Command. Between 10 p.m. and 1 a.m. slight gas shelling of Reserve bay area. Wired south side BARTS ALLEY. 23rd NORTHUMBERLAND FUS. not reconnoitring position round line known to relieving on 29th.	A.9.Q.Q

LIEUT.-COL.
COMMANDING 14th Bn. LEICESTERSHIRE REG.

SECRET

Army Form C. 2118.

WAR DIARY
or
INTELLIGENCE SUMMARY. 14th LEICESTER Rs.

(Erase heading not required.)

Place	Date Aug 1918	Hour	Summary of Events and Information	Remarks and references to Appendices
G.2.d.0.0	29th		Quiet day. Relief by 23rd Northumberlands cancelled, battn to be relieved by 18th Leicesters after on 31st.	MPQ
GORRE MAP 1/20,000.	30th		Quiet day, fine weather. Intermittent gas shelling during night.	MPQ
do	31		Bn relieved by 18th Leicesters Rifles. Relief commenced 10am for A + D coys. 2pm for B + C coys MQ. Relief complete by 5.15 p.m. Battn billetted in huts in NOEUX-LES-MINES. K.24.B.9.7. and 44 B.1/4000	

[signature]
LIEUT.-COL.
COMMANDING 14th Bn. LEICESTERSHIRE REGT.

Copy No. 12.

14th, Leicestershire Regiment.

Battalion Order No. 1.   11.8.18

1. The Battalion will move to day by route to THUBEAUVILLE and ENGUINEHAUT area.

2. Battalion Headquarters will be established at ENGUINE-HAUT.
   A & B Coys: will be billeted at THUBEAUVILLE.
   C & D "   "   "   "   " ENGUINEHAUT.
   Quartermasters Stores and Transport at ENGUINEHAUT.

3. Baggage wagons are allotted to each half Battn.

4. Coys: will move under own arrangements any time after 6.0 pm today. Coys: will report as soon as they arrive in new area.

5. Before leaving present area, all billets must be left in a clean and tidy condition, and one Officer per Coy: will be detailed by Os.C Coys: to inspect billets before marching off.

                                  (sd) H.G.Oxley, Capt & Adjt:

11.8.18   14th, Leicestershire Regiment.

Issued by runner at 3.45 pm.

  Distribution:-

     Copy No.1.   To   C.O.
          2   A Coy:
          3.   B "
          4.   C "
          5.   D "
          6   H.Q. "
          7   Q.M.
          8   T.O.
          9   Officers' Mess.
         10   Retained.
         11   "
         12   War Diary

SECRET.   Copy No....8........

14th. LEICESTERSHIRE REGT. ORDER No.2.

18th. August 1918.

Ref.1/100,000 map CALAIS HAZEBROUCK and LENS sheets.

1. The 47th Infy. Bde. will proceed to 1st Corps area on 18/19th inst:

2. The Battalion will move tomorrow 19th August 1918 by bus to NOEUX - LES - MINES area Transport will proceed by march route today Aug: 18th under Capt: PATCHETT, 143rd Coy: A.S.C. as per attached table.

3. HQ, C & D Coys: will parade at Bn. Hqrs. 5.50 am. 19th August ready to march to embussing point 800x S.W. H of HODICQ.
A & B Coys: will move off at 6.15 am., from THUBEAUVILLE and meet remainder of Battn. at road junction about 400x N of T in PARENTY at 7.0 am approx. Order of march will then be HQ,C,D,A,& B Coys:
Transport will parade under T.O. in the road S of Transport Lines at 4.15 pm. 18th inst: and will pass Brigade point CROSS ROADS 500x N.W. of E of ENQUIN at 5.11 pm.

4. Coys: will take Lewis guns and 20 filled magazines per gun with them, when embussing, but not the boxed reserve of S.A.A. Guns will be packed in the Golf bags. Gun boxes should be taken in limbers. Iron rations, rations for 19th and 20th and 120 rds. S.A.A. will be carried on the man.
Dress:- F.S.M.O., steel helmets on pack, soft caps to be worn, Box respirators slung.
Stretcher bearers will not carry rifles.

5. P.and B.T. Instructors will proceed with Battalion. Interpreter will proceed with Transport.

6. XXXXXXXXXXXXXXXXXXXXXXXXXXXXXXXXXXXXXXXXXXXXXX
6. ACKNOWLEDGE.

                                       (sd)   H.G.Oxley, Capt & Adjt:
                                               14th, Leicestershire Regiment.

Issued by runner at.......

Distribution:-

         Copy No.1. to C.O.
                 2   A.Coy:
                 3   B "
                 4   C "
                 5   D "
                 6   Q.M.
                 7   T.O.
                 8   War Diary.
                 9   Retained.

SECRET.   Copy......11......

              14th, Leicestershire Regiment Order No.3.
Ref.1/20,000 map GORRE 2nd edition.   20.8.18

   1. The Battalion will relieve 1st.Bn. Gloucester
      Regt: tomorrow Aug: 21st in the HOHENZOLLERN SECTION.
      Time of starting 9.0 am.
   2. All defence schemes, air photos, special instructions,
      list of trench stores, maps, except 1/100,000 and
      44b 1/40,000 will be handed over.
      List of trench stores and maps to reach Bn. Hqrs by
      8.0 pm 21st.

   3. Order of releif
      1st Gloucester.   14th, Leicestershires.
         H.Q. releived by   H.Q.
         D Coy: "   "   D. Coy.
         A. "   "   "   A. "
         C. "   "   "   B. "
         B. "   "   "   C. "

      Route:- L.21.a.8.8. - L.11.c.95.20.
      The following intervals will be strictly main-
      tained E. of NOEUX-LES-MINES. 300 yards bet-
      ween platoons - 500 yards between Companies - 100
      yards between vehicles, 200 yards between sections will
      be maintained beyond NOYELLES.
      Guides from 1st Gloucesters, 1 per Coy: H.Q., 1 per
      platoon, 1 for Bn.Hqrs. will be at NOYELLES
      L.11.c.95.20 at 10.30 am.
      Lewis gun limbers will report to Coy: HQrs at 8.30 am.
      to carry Lewis guns, Officers trench bundles, and
      Coy: dixes. They will march in front of Coys: and will
      not proceed East of NOYELLES - ANNEQUIN Cross roads.
      These limbers will wait to take back Lewis guns out-
      going Battn. to embussing point at K.28.a.8.7.
      Surplus personnel as detailed will collect at B.H.Q.
      under Leiut: Grant and march to Reception Camp Q.8
      central.
      All surplus kit not for line will be dumped at Bn.Hq.
      by 8.30 am. Lieut: Grant will make arrangements with
      the Q.M. for transporting this to Q.M. Stores.
      Relief complete will be notified by Coy: Commanders
      name.

   4. ACKNOWLEDGE.
                                    (sd) H.G.Oxley, Capt & Adjt:

                                    14th, Leicestershire Regt:

Distribution.
Copy No.1. to Brigade.   Copy No.8. to T.O.
     2.   1st Gloucesters.   9.   Lieut: Grant.
     3.   A Coy: 10.   H.Q.
     4.   B "   11.   War Diary.
     5.   C "   12.   Retained.
     6.   D "
     7.   Q.M.

SECRET.   Copy No. 10

14th. Leicestershire Regiment Order No.4.

Reference 1/20,000 map GORRE 2nd Edition.   30th August 1918.

1. The Battalion will be relieved by the 18th Scottish Rifles in the Right Sub-Section on August 31st.
   A & B Coys: will be relieved in the morning. Relief to be complete by 12.0 noon.
   B & C Coys: will be relieved in the afternoon. Relief to commence 2.0 pm.
   On relief the Battalion will be accomodated in NOEUX-LES-MINES.

2. All trench stores, defence schemes, tracings and trench maps (except GORRE Sheets) Air Photographs, Intelligence files, working parties will be carefully handed over. Lists of trench stores to reach B.H.Q. by 9.0 am. Sept 1st.

3. Order of Relief:-

14th Leicesters.	18th. Scottish Rifles.
A Coy:	No.1 Coy:
D "	" 4 "
Hdqrs.	Hdqrs.
B Coy:	No.2. Coy:
C "	" 5 "

   <u>Guides.</u> 1 per platoon, 1 per Coy: Hqrs, will be sent by A & D Coys: to NOYELLES Cross Roads, L.11.c.95.20 at 10.0 am. Guides from Hqrs, B & C Coys: to be at same place at 2.0 pm. Route to be followed:- Cross roads - BULLY KEEP - Route 2.
   One limber per Coy: and 1 for Hqrs., will be waiting at Cross roads for stores and Lewis Guns.

4. The following intervals will be observed:- East of NOYELLES 200 yds. between sections, Coy: HQ to count as a platoon. East of NOEUX-LES-MINES 500 yds. between Coys: 300 yrds. between platoons & 100 yrds. between vehicles. Lewis gun limbers will march in rear of Coys:

5. One guide per Coy: will be at Cross Roads L.19.a.2.8 to conduct Coys: to billets, This is being arranged by Major S.T.Whitemore.

6. Echelon "B" will report to Bn. 4.0 pm 31st at NOEUX-LES-MINES.

7. Completion of relief will be notified to B.H.Q. by the Coy: Commanders' name. All Coy: Commanders will report in person to B.H.Q. as they leave the trenches.

8. ACKNOWLEDGE.

                                       (sd) H.G.Oxley, Capt & Adjt:
<u>Distribution:-</u>   14th Bn. Leicestershire Regiment.
Copy No.1 to 18th Scottish Rifles.
    2-5   Companies.
    6   Major S.T.Whitemore.
    7.   Quartermaster.
    8.   Lieut: A.G.Grant.
    9.   Headquarters.
    10.   War Diary.
    11-12 Reta.

SECRET.

Army Form C. 2118.

WAR DIARY
or
INTELLIGENCE SUMMARY. 14th LEICESTER. REGT.

(Erase heading not required.)

Instructions regarding War Diaries and Intelligence Summaries are contained in F.S. Regs., Part II. and the Staff Manual respectively. Title pages will be prepared in manuscript.

Vol 2

Place	Date	Hour	Summary of Events and Information	Remarks and references to Appendices
Sheet 44. B¹/140,000	1918			
NOEUX-LES-MINES K.24.a.5.5.	Sept 1	11a.m	Training. Battn Church Parade. # Remainder of day cleaning up.	1420
do	" 2		Bathing and men cleaning up.	1420
do	" 3		Training	1420
do	" 4		Training	1420
do	" 5		Training	1420
do	" 6		Training. Received orders 5.40 p.m. to move to ANNEQUIN to relieve 9th Black Watch. Proceeded by Mark Route. Relief complete 11.55 p.m.	1420
			Battn established in FOSSÉ. F.29.C.6.2.	
ANNEQUIN	" 7		18 b.w moved into VILLAGE LINE coming under orders of 18th WELSH	1420
F.29.C.6.2.			Orders received to relieve 18th SCOTTISH RIFLES in Rt.SUB-SECTION	
do	" 8		Relieved 18th SCOTTISH RIFLES. 2 Companies in morning, 2 Companies in afternoon. 1420	
			relief complete 4.55 p.m. Active patrolling carried out. 11.30 p.m - 2.30 a.m	
			5 a.m - 7 a.m. all patrols entered German lines	
Sheet 44A. G.2.C.8.1.	" 9		Quiet day. Broken weather. Maintenance work carried out. Patrols out	1420
			during night as before.	

SECRET

Army Form C. 2118.

WAR DIARY
or
INTELLIGENCE SUMMARY.   14th LEICESTER REGT.

(Erase heading not required.)

Instructions regarding War Diaries and Intelligence Summaries are contained in F.S. Regs., Part II. and the Staff Manual respectively. Title pages will be prepared in manuscript.

Place	Date	Hour	Summary of Events and Information	Remarks and references to Appendices
Sheet 44.A. 1/40,000	1918 Sept			
GORRE Sheet 1/20,000	10.		Quiet day. Very windy, some rain. Patrolling carried out as usual. 5.30 am to 6.15 am Enemy bombarded our lines SOS. Gas Patrols into German lines.	1.&2.Q.
G2&C.6.1	11		Recd news that 18th Scottish Rifles relieve Bn this tomorrow.	1.Q.
do	12		Relieved by 18th Scottish Rifles relief commenced 8am complete 12.15pm 2.Q. Bn moved to ANNEQUIN.	1.Q. & 2.Q.
ANNEQUIN Sheet 44 A. 1/40,000	13.	4.25 am	Received orders for 3 companies to move forward into RT-SUB-SECTION. HQ established at G.2.C.8.1. Rest 44A. Enemy retired to Lindrick ST LAURENT line.	1.Q.
GORRE Sheet 1/20,000 G.2.&.8.1	14		Quiet day. Recd news to relieve 18th Scottish Rifles tomorrow.	1.Q.
do	15.		Relieved Scottish Rifles in RT. SUB SECTION. A Coy in FOSSE 8 area. B coy in CLIFFORD CRATERS area. C coy in support in old British line. relief complete 11.50pm. BnHQ established.	1.Q.
	16		Worked on MULE TRACK. also making runner track to forward posts. 2C Coy carried wire up for wiring A Coys posts.	1.Q.

R.W.

SECRET

Army Form C. 2118.

Instructions regarding War Diaries and Intelligence Summaries are contained in F. S. Regs., Part II. and the Staff Manual respectively. Title pages will be prepared in manuscript.

WAR DIARY
or
INTELLIGENCE SUMMARY: 14th Leicester Regt
(Erase heading not required.)

Place	Date	Hour	Summary of Events and Information	Remarks and references to Appendices
GORRE SHEET 1/20000 G.	Sept 1918 17		Quiet day intermittent hostile shelling, worked on improving tracks posts	HQ
	18		Later any relief. B. Coy relieved a D relieved B. Patrol led by 2/Lt BLACKTON reached ST. LAURENT HULLUCH line, found it strongly held, discovered M.G. position in GIBBON TR.	HQ
	19.		Quiet day. 2/Lt. BLACKTON took out fighting patrol to try repeating M. Gun in GIBBON TR. Enemy put down light barrage. Casualties NIL	HQ
	20.		Enemy artillery fairly active Barrage in front coy at 10.20am support continues stood to. Weak attack developed S of our sector became later in support	HQ
	21		Relieved by 9th Black Watch in forward area, became later in support. PHQ at FOUNTAIN KEEP G.2.c.8.1.	
G.2.c.8.1.	21.		Men spent day cleaning up, prepared for relieved by 7/6 K.O.S.B.	HQ
do	22.		Relieved by 7/8 K.O.S.B. of 15 Division, marched to SAILLY-LABOURSE. Entrained E from for LOZINGHEM. Sheet 44.B. Lilletier 11 pm.	HQ
LOZINGHEM C.18.C. Sheet 44.B. 1/40000	23.		Spent day cleaning up, refitting bathing	HQ

signature

SECRET

Army Form C. 2118.

WAR DIARY
or
~~INTELLIGENCE~~ SUMMARY. 14/LEICESTERS REGT

(Erase heading not required.)

Instructions regarding War Diaries and Intelligence Summaries are contained in F. S. Regs., Part II. and the Staff Manual respectively. Title pages will be prepared in manuscript.

Place	Date	Hour	Summary of Events and Information	Remarks and references to Appendices
Sheet 44 B 1/40000	1918 Sept			
LOZINGHEM C18C	24		Training and Bathing	1/2FO
do	25		Training. 2 companies moved to MARQUEFFEES.F.M. to take part in demonstration attack with tanks.	1/2FO
do	26		Training. Platoon football matches during afternoon	1/2FO
do	27		Training. A & B companies musketry on range in D.26.d. Battn concert 6.30pm	1/2FO
do	28		Training. Platoon football matches during afternoon	
	29		Church Parade. Capt. & Adjt H.G. Utley proceeded on leave	
	30		Training, addition of Lewis gun to battalion system of fire	

SECRET.   Copy No............

14th Bn. Leicestershire Regiment Order No. 3.

Ref. GOBRE MAP. 1/20,000.

1. The Battalion will move to ANNEQUIN LOCALITY DEFENCES.

2. Starting Point:- RAILWAY BRIDGE I.7.c.8.2
   Order of March - Hqrs, B,C,D, and A Coys:

   300 yards to be kept between platoons to Starting Point.
   200 yards between Sections EAST of Starting Point.

   Starting Point to be passed by Hqrs., at 8.30 pm.
   Leave Camp - 8.10 pm., Other Companies to follow.

3. ROUTE:- SAILLY LABOURSE - to ANNEQUIN FOSSE, where guides will meet Companies.

4. Each Company attach two guides to Headquarters.

   Dress:- as detailed.

   Rations:- As far as possible on the man, remainder on Field Kitchens. One limber per Coy: and one for Headquarters will report to Camp for Lewis guns and stores.

   D Company will leave one Lewis gun in Camp.

   20 drums per gun to be taken.

5. ACKNOWLEDGE.

                                    (sd) H.C.OXLEY, Capt: & Adjt:

                                    14th Bn. Leicestershire Regiment.

Distribution:-

   Copy No. 1 to A Coy:
        2   B "
        3   C "
        4   D "
        5   Battalion Headquarters.
        6   Quartermaster.
        7   Transport Officer.
        8   War Diary.
        9   Retained.

SECRET.   Copy No......... 6

14th Leicestershire Regiment Order No. 6
7.9.18

Ref. GORRE MAP 1/20,000.

1. The Battalion will relieve the 9th Black Watch in the HOHENZOLLERN RIGHT SUB-SECTION today.

2. B Coy: will occupy RAILWAY POST and GLOSTER POSTS.
   C Coy:- SUSSEX and WILSON, FACTORY and HUMANITY POSTS.
   A Coy:- VILLAGE LINE RIGHT.
   D "   VILLAGE LINE LEFT.

3. Order of reliefs:- B Coy, C Coy, A Coy, D Coy, and Bn. Hqrs.

   Starting Points:- Cross Roads L.5.b.central.

   Times for passing starting point:-
   B Coy:-   1.0 pm.
   C "   2.0 pm.
   A "   3.0 pm.
   D "   4.0 pm.
   Bn.Hqrs.   5.0 pm.

   Intervals of 200 yards between sections to be maintained from time of leaving billets.
   Route:- Cross roads L.5.b.central - L.6.a.2.2 (X roads) - RAILWAY L.6.a.4.8 - Track South of RAILWAY - BRAY KEEP.

   1 guide per platoon will meet Coys: at Black Watch Hqrs.

4. ALL MAPS, (except GORRE SHEET) TRENCH STORES, AIR PHOTOS, DEFENCE SCHEMES Etc., will be carefully taken over. List of stores taken over to be sent to B.H.Q. by 9.0 am. Sept. 8th.
   ALL fullerphones will be taken over from outgoing Unit.
   Each Company will take into the line 4 Dixies and Frying utensils.

4a. Code for relief complete:- Coy: Commanders' name.

5. ACKNOWLEDGE.

(sd) H.G.OXLEY, Capt: & Adjt:

14th Leicestershire Regiment.

Distribution. Issued by runner at 12.1.0. pm.

Copy No.1 to   9th Black Watch.
     2/5   Coys,
     6/7   War Diary.
     8   Headquarters.
     9   File.

SECRET.   Copy No......8....

14th Leicestershire Regiment Order No. 7.   11.2.18.

Ref. Map. GORRE 1/20,000 2nd Ed.

1. The Battalion will be relieved by 18th Scottish
    Rifles in the Right Sub-section on 12th inst:
    Relief to be complete by 1.0 pm.
    On relief the Battalion will proceed to ANNEQUIN
    DEFENCES with one company in VILLAGE LINE

2. On relief Coys: will be in following positions:-
        D Coy:-   VILLAGE LINE.
        C Coy:-   LEFT COY:
        B Coy:-   MINE KEEP.
        A Coy:-   RIGHT COY:
        B.H.Q:-   B.H.Q.
    Orders for relief as above.

3. D Coy:(Reserve) will be relieved by No.2 Coy:)will re-
    C " (Rt.Front)   "   "   "   "   " 3 ")lieve at
)same time.
    B " (Lt.Front)   "   "   "   "   " 4 ")will re-
    A " (Support)   "   "   "   "   " 1 ")lieve at
)same time.
    B.H.Q.   "   "   "   "   B.H.Q.
    D Coys: relief will leave VILLAGE LINE at 8.0 am.
    C   "   "   "   "   "   ANNEQUIN   " 8.0 am.
    A & B "   reliefs "   "   "   "   " 10.0 am.

4. Guides will be arranged as follows:-
    (1 per platoons and 1 for Coy:Hqrs.)
    From No.2 Coy: to be at D.Coys: Hqrs at 8.0 am.
    No other guides are necessary.
    Routes. C and A Coys: will use BARTS ALLEY VILLAGE LINE
            Route 2.
            B Coy: will use QUARRY ALLEY - Route 3.
    Os. C Coys: will send representatives to take over
    from their opposite numbers at ANNEQUIN and VILLAGE
    LINE. Fatigue parties with dinner etc., will move off
    in time to cook dinners at ANNEQUIN and VILLAGE LINE.
    All Companies at ANNEQUIN will move straight to their
    "stand to" positions, and will not be dismissed to
    billets until O.C. Coy: has inspected them.
    O.C. D Coy: will report to O.C. 18th Welsh Regt: when
    in position.
    Intervals of 200 yards between sections will be main-
    tained until billets are reached.

5. The following will be carefully handed over:-
        (a) All Trench Stores.
        (b) Defence Schemes, Tracing, Trench Maps (except
            GORRE sheets).
        (c) Air Photographs and Intelligence files.
        (d) Working parties, (except those permanently
            attached to R.E.).
    List of Trench stores to reach B.H.Q.by 6.0 pm 12th.

6. Completion of relief will be notified by Coy. Commanders
    name.
                                (sd) H.G.OXLEY, Capt:& Adjt:

7. ACKNOWLEDGE.
                                14th Leicestershire Regiment

SECRET. Copy No..... 7

14th Leicestershire Regiment Order No.8. 13.9.18.

Ref. GORRE. SHeet 1/20,000.

1. The three Companies of the Battalion at ANNEQUIN will move to RIGHT SUB-SECTION AREA at 5.30 am.

2. B Coy: will occupy LEFT FRONT COY: AREA.
   A "   "   "   SUPPORT"COY:"AREA (CENTRAL KEEP).
   C "   "   "   RESERVE COY: AREA.
   B.H.Q. " be at OLD HEADQUARTERS near FOUNTAIN KEEP.
   G.2.d.0.0

3. B Coy: will move at 5.30 am today 13th inst: by ROUTE 3.

4. A Coy: will move at 5.45 am by ROUTE 2.
   C "   "   "   " 5.45 am.by ROUTE 3.
   H.Q. will move at 6.0 am by ROUTE 2.
   Distance 200 yards will be maintained between platoon

4. Coys: will report to B.H.Q. G.2.d.0.0 by runner when in position.

5. Dixies etc., will be taken forward for cooking.

6. All spare kit not required will be sent to present B.H.Q. at once and left under the charge of 1 man per Coy:

7. ACKNOWLEDGE.

(sd) H.G.OXLEY, "Capt: & Adjt.

14th Leicestershire Regiment.

Distribution.

Issued by runner at 5.0 am.

Copy No.1/3 to A,B, and C Coys:
    4   Headquarters.
    5   Quartermaster.
    6/7   War Diary.
    8   File.

Distribution.

Issued by runner at ....pm.

Copy No. 1 to 18th Scottish Rifles.
         2/5 Companies.
         6   Headquarters.
         7.   Q.M.
         8/9 War Diary.
         10. File.

SECRET.   Copy No........

14th, Leicestershire Regiment Order No.9   15.9.18

Ref. AUCHY MAP No.5 1/10,000

1. The Battalion will relieve the 18th Scottish Rifles in the HOHENZOLLERN Rt. SUB-SECTION tonight Sept.15th.

2. D Coy will relieve the Coy: at present occupying OLD RT. FRONT COY: AREA. Relief to commence 3.0 pm.
   C Coy: will relieve B Coy: 14th LEICESTERS in OLD LEFT FRONT COY: AREA.
         1 platoon at DAILY POST.
         1   "   in Posts L.9a., L.10.
         2   "   " QUARRY TUNNEL.
   C Coy: to enter OLD LEFT COY: AREA at 6.0 pm.
   A Coy: will take over FOSSE 8 AREA leaving via L.5 at 7.30 am.
   B Coy: will take over CLIFFORD CRATER AREA leaving via L.2 at 7.30 pm.

3. ROUTES. D Coy: via VILLAGE LINE- BARTS ALLEY.
             C Coy: via QUARRY ALLEY.
             A Coy: via BARTS ALLEY, BARTS TUNNEL, then overland to L.5.
             B Coy: via RESERVE TRENCH, BARTS ALLEY, SAVILLE TUNNEL, L.2
   GUIDES. 1 per Coy: & 1 per platoon will be at posts L.2. and L.5 for B & A Coys: respectively at 7.30 pm.

   S.A.A.
         Each man of A & B Coys: will take an extra 50 rds. S.A.A. per man.
   GAS RATTLES & FANS should be taken forward by Companies.
   Rifle grenades A & B Coys: will take forward 2 boxes No.35s.
   Tools. Rifle sections of A & B Coys: will carry 1 shovel per man.

4. RELIEF COMPLETE will be notified by code word "BUGGER".
   Os.C.A & B Coys: when they are in position and satisfied with posts, will report to their opposite number, who will then withdraw his men.

5. ACKNOWLEDGE.

                                      (sd) H.G.Oxley. Capt & Adjt
                                        14th, Leicestershire Regiment.

Distribution:-
  Issued by runner at......pm.

  Copy No.1   18th Scottish Rifles.
       2/5   Companies.
       6   Headquarters.
       7   Quartermaster.
       8/9   War Diary.
       10   File.

SECRET.   Copy No. 6

14th Bn. Leicestershire Regiment Order No.10.   12.9.18

Ref. map AUCHY (5).

1. The following inter-company relief will take place in
   the RIGHT SUB-SECTION tonight Sept: 12th:-
       C Coy: will relieve A Coy:
       D "   "   "   B "
   Relief to commence as soon as possible after rations
   are up. 10.0 pm approx.

2. Details of relief will be arranged between Os.C Coys:
   concerned.

3. **Rations.** C and D Coys: will draw their rations before
   relieving. A and B Coys: will send advance party to
   take over rations at Dump, until relief is complete.
   Water. A and B Coys: on relief will arrange to carry
   forward water supply to C and D Coys:
   S.A.A. C and D Coys: will each take forward 4 boxes
   S.A.A. (1 per post) as reserve. D Coy: to draw from
   SAVILLE Dump.
   Socks. Clean socks are being sent up with rations
   tonight for A and B Coys: Dirty socks will be collected and sent to Q.M.Stores tomorrow night Sept.19th
   by returning ration train.

4. D Coy: must make own arrangements for hot tea to be
   taken forward during night Sept: 12/19th. Arrangements
   will be made for hot tea to be sent forward to C Coy:
   during day Sept: 19th.

5. **Patrols.** A Coy: will carry out patrol into GIBSON
   TRENCH.

6. Relief complete to be notified by code word "JOSEPHINE".

7. ACKNOWLEDGE.

                                    (sd) H.C.OXLEY, Capt: &
Distribution:-   Adjt:
   Copy No.1 to Bn.Hqrs.   14th Bn. Leicestershire Regiment.
        2/5   Coys:
        6/7   War Diary.
        8   File.

SECRET. Copy No...........

14th, Leicestershire Regiment Order No.11.   20.9.18

Ref. Map. GORRE SHEET 1/20,000.

1. The 9th Black Watch will relieve the Battalion in RT. SUB-SECTION today. Relief commencing 7.0 pm.
2. C Coy: are relieved by D Coy: 9th BLACK WATCH.
   D "   "   "   " B   "   "   "   "
   A and B Coys: remain in their positions and automatically pass into support on completion of relief.
3. Dispositions of Coys: on relief as per warning order of yesterday.
4. **GUIDES.** C Coy: will have guides (Q per platoon & 1 per Coy: Hqrs.) at L.10 at 7.0 pm.
   Guide will be provided at Bn. Hqrs. to take relief to L.10
   D Coy: will have guides (1 per platoon and 1 per Coy:HQ) L.2 at 7.0 pm.
   Guide from B.H.Q. will meet incoming Coy: at JUNCTION BARTS ALLEY & RESERVE TRENCH to conduct relief to L.2.
   Routes. C Coy: Incoming Coy: will relieve via QUARRY ALLEY - RESERVE TRENCH - LEFT BOYAU - L.10. C Coy: on relief will proceed via L.10.- OVERLAND TRACK to RESERVE TRENCH - then ROUTE 2.
   D Coy: Incoming Coy: will proceed via
   - BARTS ALLEY - SAVILLE ROW J SAVILLE TUNNEL - L.2 - posts. D Coy: on relief will proceed via L.2 - MULE TRACK - New area.
   Intervals. Incoming Coys: of BLACK WATCH can proceed at platoon intervals up to L.10 and L.2 and by section intervals from there to front posts. C & D Coys: on relief will proceed at section intervals to new area.
   Rations. Rations will be at VERMELLES at 6.0 pm. A & B Coys: will send ration parties to same place, near BARTS POST as when Bn. was in support. C & D Coys: will send N.C.O. to take over rations untill relief is complete.
5. The following will be carefully handed over:-
   (a) All Trench stores.
   (b) Work in progress and proposed.
   (c) Maps etc.,
   Receipts will be taken for all fullerphones & signal stores. Trench store list to reach B.H.Q. by 1.0 pm. 21st inst. A & B Coys: will also render list of stores & reserve dumps in their area.
6. Relief complete will be notified by code word "TOOTSIE"
7. ACKNOWLEDGE.

(sd) H.G.Oxley, Capt: & Adjt:

For O.C. 14th, Leicestershire Regiment:

Distribution:-
Copy No.1 to 9th Black Watch.
2/5 Coys:
6   Hqrs.
7   Q.M.
8/9   War Diary.
10   File.

SECRET.   Copy No............

                14th. Leicestershire Regiment Order No.12   22.9.18

Ref. GORRE SHEET 1/20,000.

1. 7/8th K.O.S.B. will relieve the Bn. today Sept: 22nd.
   On relief the Bn. will proceed to LOZINGHEM by bus.
2. Platoons now in Water Post will not be relieved but
   will withdraw when its Company relief is complete.
   Lewis Gun team, 1st CORPS CYCLIST Bn. at present attached
   will withdraw at 10.30 pm., Sept: 22nd, unless previously
   relieved, and will rendezvous at ANNEQUIN FOSSE I.6.a.6.9
   where transport will meet them at 11.30 pm., thence they
   will proceed to rejoin their Unit at VERQUIN. Os C Coys:
   to which these are attached are responsible that the teams
   are informed of this order.
3. Advanced parties 1 officer per Coy: & 1 N.C.O. per
   platoon will report to Coys: during the morning & will
   remain in the line untill the arrival of their Units.
4. Guides as detailed with 1 officer per Coy: in charge,
   will meet the incoming Coys:
5. The following will be carefully handed over and receipt
   taken:-
   1. All maps, plans, Air photos & documents connected with
      the line.
   2. All Trench Stores.
   3. All work in progress & proposed (in writing).
   Trench store lists to reach Bn. Hqrs. by 12.0 noon
   Sept.23rd.
6. On relief, the companies will move out at platoon
   interval of 3000x to the embussing point at NORTH CROSS
   ROADS, SAILLY LA BOURSE F.27.c.8.1 where they will
   report to Capt: T.B.Masters who is in charge of
   embussing.
   Route:- A & B Coys:- QUARRY ALLEY - ROUTE 3 to ANNEQUIN
   FOSSE, thence by track to CROSS ROADS.
         C & D Coys:- Route 2 - ANNEQUIN - SALLY
         LABOURSE ROAD - CROSS ROADS.

7. Os. C Coys: will each report relief complete, as they
   pass B.H.Q. in person.
8. ACKNOWLEDGE.
                                (sd) H.G.Oxley, Capt & Adjt:

                                14th, Leicestershire Regiment.

Distribution.

Copy No.1/4 to Coys:
         5.   Headquarters.
         6.   7/8th K.O.S.B.
         7.   Q.M.
         8/9   War Diary.
         10   File.

SECRET.   4/7/10

Army Form C. 2118.

WAR DIARY
or
INTELLIGENCE SUMMARY.
(Erase heading not required.)

14th LEICESTER REGT.

Vol 3

Place	Date 1918	Hour	Summary of Events and Information	Remarks and references to Appendices
HAZEBROUCK Sh. F.b.05.10. LOZINGHEM	Oct. 1	1000	Bnttn marched to NOEUX-LES-MINES, dinners on the march	1/10,000
NOEUX-LES-MINES	2		Training	1/10,000
44 A. K.18. 1/40,000	3		do	1/20
do	4		do	1/20
do	5		do	2/20
do	6		do	1/20
do	7		Training. Lt. Col. J.C. Barnes DSO wounded while reconnoitring line near BERCLAU 1/10,000	
			Sheet 44 A. 1/40,000 B.16	
do	8		Battn left NOEUX-LES-MINES and proceeded to VILLAGE LINE, CAMBRIN 44A. P.20.	1/20
CAMBRIN 44A Sheets A.20	9		Relieved 12th Scottish Rifles in line at BILLY, Sheet 44A 1/40,000 A.22.d + 23.c	1/20
BILLY A.22.d.	10		Quiet day. hostile M.G. activity during night. Lt. Col. W.L. de M. CAREY D.S.O. (Royal Irperiual) R.E. reported for duty and assumed command.	1/20
do	11		Quiet day. 2nd Lt. J.O. KAY M.C.O.R. patrolled at night crossing HAUTE DEULE CANAL with P.20. Our own fire opened. CAPT. G.B. OLIVIER proceeded on leave.	P.20
			Our own fire opened. 1 O.R. wounded.	

Maxy Lt. Col.
Commanding 14th Leicester Regt 1

SECRET.

Army Form C. 2118.

WAR DIARY
or
INTELLIGENCE SUMMARY.

14th LEICESTER REGT

(Erase heading not required.)

Instructions regarding War Diaries and Intelligence Summaries are contained in F. S. Regs., Part II. and the Staff Manual respectively. Title pages will be prepared in manuscript.

Place	Date 1918 Oct	Hour	Summary of Events and Information	Remarks and references to Appendices
Sheet 44A 1/40000				
BILLY B22d	12		Quiet day. Hostile MGun activity + gas shelling during night. 1 OR wounded	1hr20
do	13		Battn relieved by 18th Welsh Regt. Battn proceeded to ROBERTSONS TUNNELS.	2hr00
NEW CAMBRIN A20c	14		1 OR wounded	
do			Battn bathed. Inspections under Coy arrangements	7hr20
do	15		Bathing continued. 1545 Battn moved to BILLY. Enemy retiring withdrawn. Capt C.H. GREAVES, Lt & Qm J. WITHERS DCM proceeded on leave.	1hr00
BILLY B22d	16	0900	Battn moved to BAUVIN C19d, and at 1400 moved to PROVIN C27A/C Capt + Adjt H.G. OXLEY reported from leave Capt T.R. MASTERS proceeded on leave.	1hr00
PROVIN C27A/c	17	0600	Battn moved from PROVIN to BAUVE-de-CARVIN(C17c) and at 1100 pushed through to CAMPHIN, D27A, thence to PHALEMPIN, D23. Coyd established at D23.b.6.4. Battn passed through 9th BLACK WATCH took over outpost line. A, D + B coys in front line, b. coy in support.	

O.C. 14 Leicester Regt

Army Form C. 2118.

WAR DIARY
or
INTELLIGENCE SUMMARY.
(Erase heading not required.)

Instructions regarding War Diaries and Intelligence Summaries are contained in F. S. Regs., Part II. and the Staff Manual respectively. Title pages will be prepared in manuscript.

Place	Date 1916 Oct	Hour	Summary of Events and Information	Remarks and references to Appendices
D23 Sheet 44A 1/40000 PHALEMPIN	18	0800	Battn moved as Southern Advance guard of Division towards PONT A MARCQ reaching Western edge 0930. Few enemy M.G. detachments reported holding town. Battn passed through town. Recy detachments sent from F15 to F21. Recy an outpost A-C in reserve. Bn HQ established at F19.c.9.7 about 1230. At 1500 outpost moved forward. Few enemy hostile M.G. June 1640 O-B coys under Capt. G.H. GOFF moved forward and entered TEMPLEUVE (F17). Outpost line F15f - F17a.3.9 F23f.1.7 F29a.9.9 to railway F29a.3.6 F29 established F21C.1.7 in touch on flanks with 15 Division and 6th Battery 18th WELSH REGT.	A331
F21.C.1.7 Sheet 44A 1/40000	19	0640	Battn received orders to continue as Advance guard. B coy to keep through outpost line at 0900. No opposition moved on to HARDINERE to CORRIEUX. Outpost line established on road running NW-SE through B1 & C about HH 1/40000. Main body relief in CORRIEUX for dinners. Struck with Division on flanks, 12th WELSH carried out Outpost line extended N to S30 A.2.9 Sheet 37 1/40000, 2 coys in line C-A coys. B coys HQ in L.A. POSTERIE. A & C outpost HH 1/40000.	

signed
Lt Col
O.C. 14th Leicestershire Regt.

SECRET.

Army Form C. 2118.

WAR DIARY
or
INTELLIGENCE SUMMARY.   14th LEICESTER R. REGT.

(Erase heading not required.)

Place	Date 1918 Oct.	Hour	Summary of Events and Information	Remarks and references to Appendices
LA POSTERIE Sht 44/40000 A 6 c.	20	—	18th WELSH REGT take over the advance Guard of Brigade from through outpost line at 0800. 9th BLACK WATCH pass through at 0900. Battn. becomes 2nd part of Main Body. At 0940 received orders to billet in BRCHY. sheet 37/40000, T.25 central. At 1300 received orders that further advance was being made, in 2 bounds. Proceeded and found no resistance before to billet in RUMES. 2nd Batta. billet in RUMES, Bn HQ established at T.28.d.9.5. sheet 37/40000.	A69
RUMES T.28.d.9.5 Sht 37/40000	21	0915	Battn. moved to TRINTIGNIES having passed through 18th WELSH becoming support to 9th Black Watch, reached TRINTIGNIES 1045. Had dinners here eventually billet Bn HQ at 10 c.5.0 here. AYC moved to prepare to V.27.a & V.27.c Brengun in TRINTIGNIES during night. 2nd Lt Robinson & 3 O.R. wounded.	A90
TRINTIGNIES	22	2000	Rillenafferick Bath. in front line. A Coy go remain in previous positions. Prop at V.21.d.6.2. B Coy on Right front. D Coy on Left front moved to posts at 2400 during night to retain commanding position relieving Rum.	A91

Major
O.C. 14 Leicester

SECRET.

Army Form C. 2118.

WAR DIARY
or
INTELLIGENCE SUMMARY.

14th LEICESTER. REGT

(Erase heading not required.)

Instructions regarding War Diaries and Intelligence Summaries are contained in F. S. Regs., Part II. and the Staff Manual respectively. Title pages will be prepared in manuscript.

Place	Date 1918 Oct.	Hour	Summary of Events and Information	Remarks and references to Appendices
U21d6.2.	23.		Posts established by B Coy in V20 A + C. Hostile MG fire prevents patrols	AEO
Lut 37 U14d0.0.0		2140	emerging from BRUYELLES. 2140. 1 prisoner captured by D Coy in V18b a deserter. B Coy carry out patrol operation.	
do	24.		Early quiet day. relieved orders that batt. moves to be relieved by the 10th Welch. B Coy carry out small operation of clearing houses at V20C.6.3. Relief complete batt. in trenches by 0200 25th inst. Bn HQ B + D coys in	AEO
TAINTIGNIES	25	1400	TAINTIGNIES, A + C coys in LE PREAU (U20a). Battn relieved by 18th Gloucesters, moved into rest billets at PACHY	AEO
U25d6.2 PACHY T35.C.2.3.	26		BnHQ at T35.C.2.3. Fairly bathing. Interior economy organisation carried on. CAPT P.H. HILLCOAT proceeded on leave.	AEO
do	27	11.15	Church parade 11.15. A, B + C coys working on road repair during day.	AEO
do	28		Training. D coy on road repairs, remainder training	AEO

W[...] Lieut Col.
o. 14th Leicester Regt.

SECRET.

Army Form C. 2118.

WAR DIARY
or
INTELLIGENCE SUMMARY.

14th LEICESTER REGT

(Erase heading not required.)

Place	Date	Hour	Summary of Events and Information	Remarks and references to Appendices
ORCHY	1918 Oct 29		Training. Major Whitmore evacuated to hospital (sick) Capt L.H. Goff	
Shut 37/40000 T25c.	30		taken over duties of 2nd in command. Training	A.120 A.121
do	31		Training	A.122

Major Lieut Col
OC 14th Leicestershire Regt

Copy No. 11

Army Form
Unit 14th Bn. Leicestershire Regiment
DAILY ORDERS. PART II. No.
4.10.18.

Ref. 1/40,000 Sheet 44b.

1. The Battalion will move from .... to NOEUX-LES-MINES
   (distance about 10 miles.)

2. Starting Point:- Cross Roads C.18.d.5.1
   Route:- Cross Roads:- J.10.b.3.5 - K.3.a.6.2

3. The battalion will pass the starting point at 1030.
   Order of March:- Bn. Hqrs, A, B, C, D Coys: Transport.
   200 yards intervals will be maintained between Companies
   and between last Coy: and Transport.
   Field Kitchens will march with Coys:
   Dress:- Fighting Order with greatcoats. Soft Caps
   will be worn.

4. The following Billeting parties will report to Bn. Hqrs.
   at 0800 to 2/Lieut: G.W.Smith:- 1 N.C.O. per Coy:
   1 Bn. Hqrs., and 1 for Q.M. Stores. Bicycles will be
   (1 for Transport) provided, and report to Town Major, NOEUX-LES-MINES
   and take over billets vacated by 34th LONDON REGT: in
   K.24.b.9.9.
   The Transport N.C.O. will meet Staff Captain at T.Ms
   Office at 1100.

5. Details.
   Dinners will be cooked enroute and taken at the halt
   East of J.11.d.0.8 when a halt will be made for one hour.
   Transport to report to Q.M. Stores at 0830.
   All kits, blankets, Orderly Room Stores and packs etc.,
   to be at Q.M. Stores at 0930.
   Loading party will be ordered by Q.M. and march with wagons
   Dinners for Headquarters will be on A Coy: Cooker &
   for Transport details on D Coy: Cooker.
   Mess Cart to report at Headquarter Mess at 0930.
   Maltese cart at R.A.P. at 0930.
   Baggage wagons will accom any units.
   1 lorry will report at 0800 at Bn. Hqrs., and will make
   2 journeys. Q.M. will send a guide for this.
   All kits, overweight and beds etc., will be dumped and
   stored and collected when possible.

6. ACKNOWLEDGE.

                                      (sd) A.S.Heywood, Lt: & A/Adjt:

Issued by runner at .....   14th Leicestershire Regiment.

Distribution:-
   Copy No.1,2,3,4,   to Coys:
            5.   Bn. Hqrs.
            6.   T.O.
            7.   Q.M.
            8.   2/Lt: Smith.
            9.   Retained.
           10/11   War Diary.

Each issue of Orders will be issued consecutively throughout the year. A fresh series to be commenced with the first issue in each year.

Army Form O...
All Arms.

Unit_____
DAILY ORDERS. PART II.   No._____

N.B.—The Sub. No. of Order and Subject are to be shown in cols. 1 and 2, thus:—1.—Courts Martial.

Station_____   Date_____

Regimental No., Rank and Name.	Sqdn., Batty. or Co.	Particulars of Casualties, etc., and Date.

Officer Commanding *or* Adjutant.

Copy No...10...

14th Leicestershire Regiment Order No.14 7.10.18.

Ref. 1/40,000 map sheet 44B

1. The Battalion will relieve 34th LONDON REGT: tomorrow Oct.8th in the VILLAGE LINE.
   O of M - Hdrs, A,B,C,D and Transport.

2. The head of Column will leave starting point L.13.c.1.8 at 1000. Route:- GATILY LABOURSE.
   Dress:- Fighting Order and Great Coats (as before)
   Steel helmets will be worn. 120 rds. S.A.A. per man will be carried. Soft caps will not be taken.
   Field cookers will march in rear of Bn. and dinners served when reliefs are completed.

3. The following advance parties will report to B.H.Q. 0730 Capt: Masters, 1 R.C.O. per Coy: and 1 for Bn.Hqrs., and will report to outgoing unit in VILLAGE LINE at 1000.

4. Blankets, packs, Orderly Room Stores etc., to be handed in to Q.M.Stores by 08.30 am., and Officers' kits by 0900.

5. Transport Lines and Q.M.Stores will be at F.29.d. Transport Officer will detail 1 N.C.O. to report to Staff Captain at F.29.c.1.5 at 1100 Oct.8th to allot Transport Lines.

6. Lorry arrangements (if any) will be notified later.

7. 200 yard intervals will be maintained between Coys: and between the last Coy: and Battalion Transport. Baggage wagons &c. will accompany Transport.

8. Coys: will render receipts for Trench Stores to B.H.Q. by 1600 Oct: 8th.

9. Relief complete will be notified by code word "TOMMY".

10. Details for Echelon B will parade B.H.Q. 0745 under R.S.M. Dress:- F.S.M.O.

11. ACKNOWLEDGE.

(sd) A.S.Heywood, Lt: & A/Adjt:
14th Bn. Leicestershire Regiment.

Issued by runner at:-
Distribution:-
Copy No.1 to Bn.Hqrs.
    2/5   Coys:
    6   Q.M.
    7   T.O.
    8   Capt:Masters.
    9/10   War Diary.
    11   Retained.

Army Form B. 231.

FIELD STATE.

Unit _____
Place _____
Date _____

To be rendered in accordance with Field Service Regulations, Part II.

FIGHTING STRENGTH.

This should *not* include details attached to unit, or personnel detailed to march with the Train, or any men unfit to go into action with unit

RATION STRENGTH

To include Fighting Strength, Personnel detailed to march with the Train, and all Personnel and animals attached for Rations and Forage

UNIT	Personnel		Horses and Mules		Other Animals	Guns and Ammunition Wagons (stating nature)	Machine Guns	Ambulances	Tool Carts, Technical Carts (stating nature)	Remarks	Personnel	Horses and Mules		Other Animals	Mechanically Propelled Vehicles				Remarks
	Officers	Other Ranks	Riding	Draught and Pack							Total, all Ranks entitled to Rations	Heavy Horses and Horses	Other Horses and Mules		Motor Cars	Motor Bicycles	Lorries 3 Ton	Lorries 30 Cwt.	Tractors	
(1)	(2)	(3)	(4)	(5)	(6)	(7)	(8)	(9)	(10)	(11)	(12)	(13)	(14)	(15)	(16)	(17)	(18)	(19)	(20)	(21)	(22)	(23)

TOTALS ...

Ammunition with Unit :—
·303 inch; approximate number of rounds per Man _____
·303 inch; ,,   ,,   ,,   per Machine Gun _____
Gun or Howitzer; approximate number } of rounds per Gun or Howitzer } _____

Supplies with Unit :—
Approximate number of days' rations for men of ration strength _____
,,   ,,   ,, forage for Animals _____
,,   ,,   ,, fuel and lubricants for Mechanically } Propelled Vehicles } _____

Signature of Commander

(2 38 4) W5265—M2509 100,000 7/17 HWV(319) [Sch. 128] Form/B.231/5

SECRET.

14th Bn. LEICESTERSHIRE REGT:

Copy No. 10

OPERATION ORDER NO.1.   15.10.18.

1. The Battalion will be held in readiness to move at one hours notice.

2. Dress:- F.S.M.O.

3. Transport will accompany the Battalion.

4. If the Battalion is ordered to the front line, packs will be dumped in the vicinity of BILLY.

5. Parades for Bathing and Medical Inspections will carry on, and will be expedited as possible.
   The M.O. will arrange direct with Company Commanders as to hours.

Issued by runner at 1215
Copy No.1   to Bn.Hqrs.
    2/5   " Coys:
    6   " T.O.
    7.   " M.O.
    8/9   " War Diary.
    10   " Retained.

(sd) T.B.Masters,Capt:& A/Adjt:
14th Leicestershire Regiment.

SECRET.   Copy No............

14th LEICESTERSHIRE REGT.

OPERATION ORDER NO.2 15.10.18

1. Battalion, less A Coy: will move to CITIE DE DOUVRIN under Coy: Commanders at 1545. A Coy: will follow after bathing.

2. Order of March:- C,D,B Coys, Bn.Hqrs. and A Coy:

3. Dress:- F.S.M.O.

4. <u>Transport.</u> Lewis gun limbers will report to their respective Coys: immediately. Water carts and Cookers will proceed to new billeting area immediately on receipt of these orders. Mess cart and 1 limber for Bn.Hqrs. will report to level crossing of light railway on CAMBRIN-LA BASSEE ROAD immediately. Maltese cart to report to R.A.P. at once.
Guides will meet Battalion at B.19.a.30.20

Issued by runner at 1450   (sd) T.B.Masters, Capt: &
Copy No.1 to Bn.Hqrs.   A/Adjt:
    2/5 Coys:
    6   T.O.
    7   M.O.
    8/9 War Diary.
    10   Retained.

14th Leicestershire

Operation Orders No 4.

Warning Order.

1. Our line now runs through C.9.C. C.15.B. C.21.d. and patrols are going forward to ANNOEULLIN.

2. The Battalion will be in readiness from dawn 16th to move at half an hours notice to pass through the front line battalion, and take up the pursuit of the enemy.

3. A. B. Coys will be in front of C & D in support.

4. <u>Dress</u>, Fighting order without greatcoats 120 rounds per man
                  16 magazines per L.Gun.

5. Packs will be dumped as follows:
           B.E.
       A C & D Coys Bn Hqrs. BERCLAU
    A & B C will each leave a man in charge of their dumps.

6. Field Kitchens will follow in rear of Battn Hqrs under the Sgt Cook. Men will carry a proportion of the Biscuit ration.
Water bottles will be filled before starting.

7. Transport is marching from ANNEQUIN to BILLY at 0930.

A B C D. Coys.
M.O
ADST
File.

Secret   Copy No.

14R. Leicestershire Regt.
Operation Order No 6.   16-10-18.

Warning Order

1. The 2-nd objective from D.У.a to D 25 central has been occupied by the 9th Black Watch.

2. On Battalion will be in readiness to move this afternoon to the following positions:-

      A & C Coys. ANNOELLIN
      B & D Coys. PROVIN

                         Lieut Col.
                Comd 14th Leicestershire Regt.

14th Leicestershire Regt.

Operation Order No 7.   17-10-18.

1. The Bn will march immediately to CAMPHIN, under Coy arrangements. Distances of 100 yds between platoons will be maintained.

2. Dinners will be served 1230. Field Cookers will join Coys at CAMPHIN.

3. The Bn will be ready to move further at 1400.

4. Instructions will be sent from B.H.Q giving detailed orders.

Major
14th Leicestershire Regt.

1/4R Leicester Regt.
Operation Orders No 8.

1. At dawn 47 Bde will make good line CANIPHIN-CHEMY-CROISETTE, and continue advance to 41R objective, LABEUVRIERE-PHALEMPIN-LESEPINCHEUSES thence railway to northern boundary.

   Reft of 15R Divn is advancing to high ground THUMEQOIES- K-7 - D. 30 D.0.0

   55R Divn are clearing GONDECOURT and BOIS de LHOSQUE at dawn.

   Left flank of 47R Bde will be refused to effect junction with 55 Divn.

   TAKU moves forward 1500 yds in rear of MON.

2. TECU will move to line C 29 central C 23 antia

       A Coy on left with C. Coy in support
       B. Coy on right with D Coy in support

       A & B Coys will march at 0800
       C & D Coys & Bn Hqs at 0815

3. Formation platoons in fours at 200 paces distance

4. Route. across open

5. Dress. Fighting order without greatcoats, 120 rounds per man, 16 magazines per L.G.

6. Packs will be dumped in Coy dumps in vicinity of Batt Hqs
   2nd in Command will select site of dumps.

7. Transport. One pack animal with each coy, carrying 2 boxes S.A.A.
   Field kitchens & mattoc Cart will follow Batt Hqs.
   The remainder now with the Battalion will remain in PROVIN till further orders.

Secret.   14th Bn. Leicestershire Regt.   Copy No.

Operation Order No.10.   18-10-18.

Ref. Map. Sheet- 44 A. 1/40,000

1. 47th Inf Bde will form the advance guard for the 16th Division, on the 19th inst. Two routes will be followed, each with a separate advance guard.

2. Southern advance guard under the Command of the O.C 14th. Leicestershire Regt will consist of 1/2 troops King's Edward's Horse, 1 section 156 Coy R.E., 471 TMB (as working party) detachment of 51st Australian Tunneling Coy (mine detectors), 1 section A Coy M.G. Bn. Section of R.F.A. One Battalion infantry.

3. Starting point will be the road junction E.14.d.2.3 First Unit to pass this point at 0800, remainder will follow at undermentioned intervals, O of M – 1/2 troops K.E.H., 1 platoon D.Coy extended at 50 paces, 500 yds interval, three platoons D.Coy with section M Guns, 100x interval, section R.E. and 471 T.M.B. 500' interval B.Coy. Section R.F.A. Battn Hqrs. A Coy & C. Coy. Route Road junction E.15.d.19. E 23 B 38 E 24 B 08 E 18 d F 2. F 190 3 8 F 21 c b 5 F 19 c 6 5.

4. Halt for dinners about 1300. Cookers will remain with Coys except D. Coy (D Coy dinners on arrival) Pack mules will go with Coys. Gun limbers will be at starting point at 0800 except C. Coy which will report C.Coy H.Q. 0700.

Fighting Order.

Welsh Regt will march on Northern Adv Guard
Route E.1.B.55 through AVELIN. ENNEVELIN F10 B central
Objective of adv Guards F.4.B.1.9. F17 central F23.d.0.5.
Boundaries between. Adv Guards line from E14 A 8 5 to F 11. C. 0. 5.
The C.O. will be with O.C. D. Coy.

5. Disposition for night 18/19 Oct
    C. Coy outpost line
    Battn H.Qrs F16. C.0.6

6. Acknowledge.
    Copy no 1/4. to A.B C D Coys
         5. to Sgt Clapshaw   8. S.O.
         6. T.O. Q.M.   9/10 W. Diary
         7. Major Whiteman   11 File

Issued to runner at-
 0105.

1/4th Leicester Regt
Operation Order No 11.

1. 4th Bde will continue its advance today. 1st objective running N and S, 1200 yds E of E edge of abt 44.A. Final objective CORBIEUX - BOIS DE CYSOING - BOIS DE LA TARSDAIER.

2. Forces will be constituted as yesterday.

3. Order of M - C Coy vanguard. M.G. section will march with vanguard, 500 yds distance RE & TMB, 500 yds distance A Coy, RFA, B Coy, D Coy. C Coy will pass through line of outposts via F.17.a - F.23.a at 0830 and make good line of railway through F.11.d - F.24.a at 0900.

4. Starting Point for main body road junction F.16.d.9.4 at 0900 Route via level crossing F.17.b.4.5 thence to F.12.a.9.8. thence GENECH (200 yds between Coys.
Bn HQrs & transport will follow in rear of main body.
Advance guard will carry 1 Lewis Gun per platoon. A Coy will carry 2 Lewis Guns in all. Remainder of Lewis Guns will be in limbers

Limbers will report to A & C Coys as soon as possible. B & D Coys limbers will report at starting point.

(Sd.) W ffo do M Carey
Lt Col

Commdg: 1: L Leicester R.g.t

14th Leicestershire Regt
Operation Order No 17. 21.10.18

1. The 147th Brigade will continue the advance tomorrow. Objective — V.18.d — V.17.a.

2. The vanguard under Lt Col Stewart DSO consisting of 9th BLACK WATCH, 1 Battery 18 pdrs, Section MGC, Platoon Corps Cyclists, will pass through present outpost line at 0900.

3. The main guard under Lt Col Carey DSO will consist of 14th Leicest Regt, 1 Battery 18 Pdrs, A Coy. 1 Section M G Coy.

4. Starting point for main guard T.29.a.2.b Time 0915. Order of March, B, Sect MG Coy, Battery 18 pdrs, D Coy, C Coy, A Coy Bn HQr. Field Kitchens & Lewis gun limbers will accompany Coys. Remainder of Transport will follow in rear under T.O. as early as possible.

5. Dress :- Marching Order.
Route. The I.O. will find out route followed by Black Watch & will direct the main guard accordingly.

(Sd) W.H. Carey Lieut Col
Comdg: 14 Leicester Regt

16th [Royal Scots?] Regt.   21/10/18.
Operation order No. 19.

                                         U17A.00
1. C. Coy. will move to ST MAUR at once
   A Coy. "   "   " LONGUESAULT
   where they will be in support to the 9th Black Watch
   H.Q. U21.D.6.2.
   Arrival to be reported both TEGU and MUNU

2. Billeting parties should be sent ahead so as to
   avoid keeping the men outside houses longer than
   necessary, as both places are frequently shelled.
   Cellars to be used where available.

3. Route. C. Coy. will not use the route through
   U23 A on account of shelling.

4. Communication will be through MUNU who has
   telephone to TEGU, and visual forwards.

5. Rations will be sent to U21.D.6.2. Coys. will
   leave guides there to bring them on. The route
   through U23A may be used by C Coys. ration limbs.

6. Lewis Guns and 16 magazines per gun will be
   taken forward (in limbers if desired) and
   limbers will be sent back to Battn. H.Q.

7. Picks only will be taken. Cookers will be sent
   back to Battn: H.Q. [struck out]

SECRET 1st Leinster Regt. Order No 21.
Sheet 57 1/40000   22-10-18
1. The Battn will relieve MUNU
   tonight.
2. B coy will take over Right
   front line. D coy left front
   line. B & D coys will report to
   MUNU HQkrs U21.d.6.2. at 2000 where
   guides will await them.
   Order of march B & D coy.
3. A & C coys on taking over as
   Reserve & support coys. orders
   already issued by C.O.
3. Field Kitchens will be left
   in present positions. also officers
   chargers, locations to be notified
   to BHQ at once.
   O.R.es will be taken.
4. S.A.A. 16 magazines per L.G.
   will be taken with Platoon.
   Balance of coy S.A.A. at Coy HQ
 * Lewis Gun limbers can go to
   MUNU HQ U21.d.6.2. or to
   MERLIN. Limbers to return

present BHQ where guide will take them to Transport lines.
5. Acknowledge.

By Runner   HQ. Only Copt
             add
17.40   for OC.
20/10/18

Copies to.   B.
             D.
             HQ. Top Text
             File.

X. Instead of M U N J. HQ
for L G Limbers read
V 23 b. 4. 7.

14th Leicester Regt
Operation Order No. ___ 23.10.17

1. Operations will be conducted tonight against enemy posts V.20.

2. 1st Objective Wood at V.20.c.88
           Pit V.20.c.9.8
   2nd Objective Pits in V.20 b + D
   3rd Objective line from V.20.a.6
           Bridge head V.20.c.3.9

3. The artillery, M.Gs 6" T.M. will shoot on all targets except V.20.c.88 up to 1830 at which time B Coy should have troops in readiness to enter 1st Objective.
   B Coy will be responsible for mopping wood at V.20.c.88 with 6 fire
   HQrs, B Coy, MGCo, 6 T.M. will be situated together in wood about V.20.c.1.9

OC B Coy will be in Command of all operations.

4. BHQ moves to Convent at MERLIN about v.30, b.30 at 1715. Signal will have Telephone communication with OC Coy & BHQ

5. Acknowledge.

Weverley Capt AA
for Smithed

Time
1510

Commdg 14th Leicestershire

14th Leicester Regt. Order No 25
23-10-18

Secret

SK V 34 1/4000

1. A Coy will send an officer patrol across river about V.26.B.2.4

2. The R.E. officer will bring boats, ropes to V.26.a.4.6 at midnight 23/24 and will superintend launching crossing.

3. 1st objective stream at V.27.a.0.9 information as to width, depth required.
   2nd objective cross stream and patrol far bank up to bridge at V.21.C.3.4
   3rd objective investigate bridge at V.21.C.3.4 and return by any route to original point of crossing.

4. OC A Coy will keep in touch with B Coy until last minute to find out progress of their operations

5. Covering fire for crossing from our side of canal to be provided and party to stay in position until return of patrol

6. Remainder of A Coy will be in support to B Coy & under orders of O.C. "B" Coy.

7. Acknowledge

By Runner
1350
23-10-18

(Sd) H. G. Oxley Capt & Adjt
for O.C.
14th Leicestershire Regt

SECRET 14th Leicestershire Regt. Copy No
          Operation Order No 24.
Sheet 37 1/40,000.

1. "A" Coy will conduct operations tonight for the purpose of obtaining prisoners and of clearing the house at V.20.c, 6.3. of the enemy

2. Before moonrise men will be posted at every entrance to the building and courtyard. The OC Coy will decide how long he will wait after moonrise before entering the house. If the enemy show any signs of leaving as on previous nights, they should be attacked as they emerge, in preference to entering whilst all are inside.

3. When taken, the house will be handed over to the left platoon Comdr. of the 18th WELSH REGT and the attacking party will return to billets in accordance with relief order No. 25.

4. Covering fire will be obtained by Lewis gun firing from the row of houses at V.20.C.4.6 and also from South. - suggested site V.26.a.9.9. Platoon will be posted in support about V.25.b.8.8. 2 at least of the Lewis guns will be capable of being trained on any route of escape of the enemy.

5. OC B Coy will inform OC "A" Coy of the location of enemy guns which might fire on the party, and will lend him such guides as may be necessary.

Lieut Col
Comdg 1/4 Leicester Regt

SECRET.   Copy.

   18th Leicester Regt Order No 25
Sheet 37. 1/40000.

1. The Battn will be relieved by the 18th WELSH
Regt tonight.
   On relief the Battn will be billetted as
follows:– A & B. Coys in TAINTIGNIES C & D
Coys in LE PREAU. B.H.Q. at FLORENT
025 a 73. Billeting parties will be sent
off forthwith. Time of relief will be
notified later.

2. Dinner will be at C Coy H.Q. Time to be
notified later.

3. Coys & B.H.Q. will march back independently
Transport lines and Q.M. stores remain
in present positions.

4. The Battn will go into Rest Billets in ROMES
on 28th inst billeting parties to report to
B.H.Q. FLORENT at 0800 on 25th inst.

5. Acknowledge.

   By Runner
       15.00.
     24.10.18.
           Copies to A B C & D Coys
                     B.H.Q.
              Major Whitmore
                18th Welsh.

Secret

14th Leicestershire Regt. No 25
Ref Sheet 51/40000   25-10-18

1. Battn will move to BACHY (T.25) today 25th inst and take over billets of 18th Gloucester Regt.

2. Starting point road junction V.25.A.5.6
Order of march HQ A.B.C.D. Coys field kitchens etc
HQ will pass starting point at 1400

3. Interval of 300ᵡ between coys will be maintained E of BACHY.

4. G limbers will report to Transport Lines before 1400 & come under orders of the T.O.
Field Kitchens will proceed with Coys to the starting point they will follow in rear of the column T.O. will appoint a N.C.O. to take charge.
Officers horses will be at starting point

4. All Billets will be left thoroughly clean
O.C. C Coy & O.C. B. Coy will be responsible that the billets in LE PREAU & TAINTIGNIES have been inspected by an officer, respectively

5. T.O will make arrangements to move. Transport as per Bde orders.

6. Acknowledge.

(Sgd) H G Oxley Capt & Adjt
for O.C.

By Runner
10.15 25/10/18.

SECRET.

Army Form C. 2118.

WAR DIARY
or
INTELLIGENCE SUMMARY.

(Erase heading not required.)

14th LEICESTERSHIRE REGT

Vol 4

Place	Date 1918	Hour	Summary of Events and Information	Remarks and references to Appendices
Shet 37. 1/40000 BACHY 725.C.2.3	Nov 1		Battn carried out training. Capt Batliff assumed duties of second in command	148
do	" 2		was kept Whitmore evacuated sick 28th Oct. Training	148
do	" 3	10.00	Battn moved to ENNEVELIN by march route.	148
ENNEVELIN Shut 44A 1/40000	" 4		Day spent in cleaning of equipment. Interior economy work & company arrangements	148
F.2 B.3.2 1/40000	" 5		Battn bathed at TEMPLEUVE. Shut 44A (F.10 d.7.6). Capt Ratliff proceeded on leave UK	148
do	" 6		Training in platoon weapons, organisation, etc carried out by companies	148
do	" 7		Training. Advance guard scheme carried out by companies, received orders to move to HUVET and FRETIN areas tomorrow	148
FRETIN Shut 36 1/40000	" 8	1000 hrs	Battn moved to new area. Headquarters in HUVET LAUNDRY. One company at LA RIVE. one company LE FOURNEAU. Battery established at FRETIN. F.21 B.6.0.	148
FRETIN Shut 36 1/40000	" 9		Bombing harness for an hour. Inspecting arms to march.	148
F.21 B.8.0 1/40000	" 10		Received orders to move to ELBAIX proceeding via GENECH. Battn paraded 1000 hrs. reached new area 1430 hrs. Bttn H.Q. established. CR & Q shut up/10000	148

Comdg 14 Leicester Regt

SECRET.

2   Army Form C. 2118.

WAR DIARY
or
INTELLIGENCE SUMMARY.
(Erase heading not required.)

1/4 Leicester Regt.

Place	Date	Hour	Summary of Events and Information	Remarks and references to Appendices
EL DAIL	1918 Nov. 11		Battn. noted News received that hostilities cease at 1100 hrs today.	SEE
Det H.Q. 1/4000 Central	12.		Inspection parade by Company commanders of day dress in respect	SEE
	13.		Educational classes arranged for men	SEE
do	14.		H.Q. companies inspected by C.O. Educational classes continued	SEE
do	15.		Battn marches to GENECH by march route, being starting point at 0900/YIBO	SEE
GENECH Det H.Q. 1/4000	16.		B.H.Q. established in GENECH at GENECH CHURCH at 0900 hrs. Battn. march to TOURNIGNES, adjt. H.H.Q. 1/4000. By march route, being Battn. H.Q. established at TOURNIGNES, F26dS2.	SEE
TOURNIGNES Det H.H.A 1/4000 F26d6.2	17.	11-15	2 coys billeted in PETIT ATTICHES Church parade on CHATEAU GROUNDS. Very wet day	SEE
	18		Company parade from 0900-1000. Remainder of morning education classes	SEE
	19		One hours training carried out during morning remainder of day spent in Education & Recreation.	SEE
do	20		As per programme for 19th	SEE

Majr Lieut-Col
of 1/4 Leicestershire Regt.

Army Form C. 2118.

WAR DIARY
or
INTELLIGENCE SUMMARY.

SECRET. 14th Leicestershire Regt.

(Erase heading not required.)

Place	Date	Hour	Summary of Events and Information	Remarks and references to Appendices
TOURMIGNIES	1918 November 21		Coy Drill from 0900-1030. Education classes remainder of morning. Football series during runs during afternoon.	
do Hutted	22		ditto	
do	23		ditto	
do	24	1000	Church Parade in Camp. Brig Gen Dent was present.	
do	25		Wiring Party training from 0900-1030 hrs. Education classes. Organized salvage work carried out. A concert was held in the Orphanage Room at 1800 hours, very successful.	
do	26		Training. Education & salvage. Football in afternoon.	
do	27		Button hunt at TEMPLEUVE BUTTS.	
do	28		Education classes & salvage work continued. B Coy inspected by B.O.	
do	29		Inter Platoon company League matches arranged for football. Wiring work carried out by Coys	
do	30		Drill Education & salvage work continued. Inter Coys Rugby cup & football cup. returning 305 parts.	

O.C. 14th Leicestershire Regt.

ORIGINAL

SECRET.

Army Form C. 2118.

14th Lancers Regt.

WAR DIARY
or
INTELLIGENCE SUMMARY
(Erase heading not required.)

Place	Date	Hour	Summary of Events and Information	Remarks and references to Appendices
TOURMIGNIES	1918 Dec 1st	1000	Arrived at Winter Camp for R.H. coys at Whithem. 1130 horses at B.D. at Patk	
			ARTICLES	
Shed 444 1/40,000	2		Cleaning and Educational classes. Salvage work.	
do	3		Salvage, Inspection & salvage. Pinto played 18th Hussars at Football won 30 Nil.	
do	4	1800	Lecture by Bde Comdr on Lord Kitchener's new demobilization 150 all ranks bys attended	
do	5		Hunt turned out also Educator classes & salvage work. Russian dance	
do	6	0730	bn O inspected bn Q inspection H. Coy	
do	7	0930	bn O inspected F Coy 0930 forts Races in afternoon Lanvaers a Rules	
			day 30 wound	
do	8	1000	bn Gurd at Ludhiana Football match during afternoon	
do	9		Living lectures given + salvage carried out	
do	10	0930	bn O inspected "A" Company Remarks very as usual	

COMMANDING 14th D.L. 28 B.E. 746

SECRET — ORIGINAL

Army Form C. 2118.

WAR DIARY
or INTELLIGENCE SUMMARY
(Erase heading not required.)

Instructions regarding War Diaries and Intelligence Summaries are contained in F.S. Regs., Part II. and the Staff Manual respectively. Title pages will be prepared in manuscript.

2nd Bn. Leinster Regt.

Place	Date	Hour	Summary of Events and Information	Remarks and references to Appendices
TOURMIGNIES SHEET 44H 1/40,000	1918 December 11	0920	Bath [arrived?] over 1030 to 1300 p.m. Lecture schemes work	
do	12	1030 to 1300	Lecture. Battalion chose a Lecture. Operations [working?]	
do			party at Bush Fund by proposed Divisional [Director?] [illegible]	
do	13		Same programme as for 12th	
do	14	0900 to 1200	A.Demptis gymnastic house. 1730 to L.D. orchestra [Living?]	
do			a cry tilley business as usual. Bomb buzzed 11th Divisional Dublin	
do	15		Lecture. Parade as usual.	
do			during afternoon and wore	
do	16		All morning parade cancelled owing to weather weather continued bad	
do			[illegible] Lecture etc. [illegible]	
do	17	1730	Batn [illegible] band arrived to [illegible] [illegible] by us as usual	
do	18		company [illegible] per arrangements Battalion [illegible] as usual	
do	19		[illegible] go by rail. Band [illegible] Left 11.20 Battalion [illegible] heavy showers	
do	20		All ranks found [illegible] owing to bad weather. [illegible] [illegible]	
			[illegible] River below [illegible] [illegible]	

[signature] Lieut-Col.
Commanding 2nd Bn. Leinster Regt.

SECRET

ORIGINAL

Army Form C. 2118.

WAR DIARY
or
INTELLIGENCE SUMMARY.
(Erase heading not required.)

1/4 Leicestershire Regt.

Instructions regarding War Diaries and Intelligence Summaries are contained in F. S. Regs., Part II. and the Staff Manual respectively. Title pages will be prepared in manuscript.

Place	Date	Hour	Summary of Events and Information	Remarks and references to Appendices
TOURMIGNIES SHEET 44.A 1/40000	21	1700-1900	Platoon drill & Training of newly arrived companies & reinforcements. Exercise circus manege 1030 & 1300 hrs	App
	22		Refly from Lille M Cline to or 3 army Command nil. The Bn. Band first furnished on the Field	App
		1000hrs	Church Parade. Forest trail broken & 2000 hrs	nil
	23	1400 hrs	no event. Enemy at Mons sent messenger by eye? groups	App
	24		Same as previous to 23rd	App
	25		Xmas Day. Bluch knows 1030 hrs	"
	26		Boxing Day	"
	27	0900-1030	Enemy men arising composite shows 62 each nears	App
	28		Same as yesterday. Man arrest Port for one examined at 0.75	App
			HW Tourmignies	nil
	29	1100	Church Parade Concert Hall.	App
	30	1030	Left et Port A MARCQ 1400 all ranks start remains of Bn.	App
	31		to arrange work. Evening Concert & Cinema as usual. Dr 2000 hrs best supper sol. Boxing Hall	App

W. Mason LIEUT.-COL.
COMMANDING 1/4.Bn. LEICESTERSHIRE REGT

(17430) Wt W4500/P773 750,000 5/18 D. D. & L., London, E.C. E 2868 Forms/C2117/18.

Army Form C. 2118.

WAR DIARY
or
INTELLIGENCE SUMMARY

14th Bn LEICESTERSHIRE REGT.

Vol 6

Place	Date	Hour	Summary of Events and Information	Remarks and references to Appendices
TOURNAI	1/1/19		No parade. Inspection made for arrangements.	JBM
	2/1/19		Training & educational classes & salvage.	JBM
	3/1/19		" " Div Band gave selections	JBM
			in concert hall.	
	4/1/19		Morning as usual. Bn. played Northumberland Fusiliers	JBM
			in 2nd round of Divisional cup at TEMPLEUVE. Win for	
			Bn 5 goals to nil.	
	5/1/19		Church services in concert hall.	JBM
	6/1/19		Training as usual. salvage.	JBM
	7/1/19		" " Bn. concert party gave performance JBM	
			in Concert Hall.	
	8/1/19		Training & salvage as usual.	JBM
	9/1/19		" " Lecture by Mr Menables in	JBM
			Concert Hall. Capt. J.R. Burn proceeded on leave.	
			Capt — baptt. commanding left for leave.	JBM

WAR DIARY
or
INTELLIGENCE SUMMARY.

Army Form C. 2118.

1/4th LEICESTERSHIRE REGT.

Place	Date	Hour	Summary of Events and Information	Remarks and references to Appendices
TOURNAISIES	10/1/19		Training as usual. C.O. inspected "D" Coy.	J.B.M.
	11/1/19		" " " Lecture by 2/Lieut Emma to West Rep. R	J.B.M.
				J.B.M.
			TAXATION CAPT P+. Shew returned to duty from Hospital	J.B.M.
			Training as usual C.O. inspected "B" Coy	J.B.M.
	12/1/19		Church parade in Concert Hall. Major St. Whitmore	J.B.M.
			Lieut Anguine + 2/Lt Walder admitted to Hosp.	J.B.M.
	13/1/19		Training as usual Lieut AS Heywood + 2/Lieut Bulling	J.B.M.
			proceeds on leave	J.B.M.
	14/1/19		Training + salvage work as usual	J.B.M.
	15/1/19		" "	J.B.M.
	16/1/19		" "	J.B.M.
	17/1/19		" " Lieut Mahir proceeds	J.B.M.
	18/1/19		on leave	
			Training + lectures by 2/Lieut Emma 15th Welsh Regt or Econom- 1650	
			history of England on 19.1 Civilian R.B. Quinn Capt - 1900	
			Government 14 Leicesters	

WAR DIARY or INTELLIGENCE SUMMARY.

Army Form C. 2118.

14th Leicestershire Regt.

Place	Date	Hour	Summary of Events and Information	Remarks and references to Appendices
TOURS/FRANCE	19/1/19		Church Service	2BM
	20/1/19		Training as usual. Lieut Perry proceed on leave to UK	2BM
	21/1/19	"	"	2BM
	22/1/19	"	C.O. Inspected B Coy. Bn. Played Royal Irish Fusiliers in final of Divinal football cup	2BM
	23/1/19		Won for Bn. 2 goals to 1. Battalion was inspected by Lt Gen. Sir ARTHUR HOLLINSHED Commanding I Corps	2BM
	24/1/19		Training as usual. Lieut Blake MC proceeded on leave.	2BM
	25/1/19	"	"	2BM
	26/1/19		Church Service	2BM
	27/1/19		Training as usual	2BM
	28/1/19		Lieut B. Meade proceed on leave	2BM
	29/1/19		Training as usual. Lieut H.W. Morrison proceeded on leave	2BM
	30/1/19		Ceremonial parade	2BM
	31/1/19	"	Captain N.G.G Riley proceeded on leave	2BM

E.T. O'Brien Capt
Commanding 14th Leicester

SECRET

WAR DIARY
or
INTELLIGENCE SUMMARY.
(Erase heading not required.)

Army Form C. 2118.

14th LEICESTERSHIRE REGT

Place	Date	Hour	Summary of Events and Information	Remarks and references to Appendices
TOURMIGNIES	1919 Sept			
	2nd		Church parade as usual.	
	3rd	10.00	Brigade ceremonial parade for presentation of colours to 1. R. of the Rouse	
			By Major K.G.	
	4th	0900-0930	Drill + Physical Training. Remainder of morning as usual.	
	5th	0900-0930	Drill + Physical Training. Morning as usual. Lt Col Ewing present 1920	
			on leave. Capt E. B. Oliver M.C. resumed command.	
	6		Usual programme of Routine.	
	7	0900-0930	Drill + Physical Training. Remainder of morning, college work.	
	8		Drill etc. Educational classes, college work carried out during morning there	
	9		Church Parade as usual.	
	10	0900-0930	Drill Physical Training. Remainder of morning as usual.	
			2Lt W Bryson proceeded on leave.	
	11		Training, Education + college as usual. Remainder during Hours	
	12		Ditto.	
	13		2Lt. L J North proceeded on leave. Routine as usual	
	14	0900-0730	Drill Physical Training under my arrangements. Remainder of the	
			day as usual.	

E B Oliver Capt
O/C 14 Leicesters

Secret

Army Form C. 2118.

Instructions regarding War Diaries and Intelligence Summaries are contained in F.S. Regs., Part II. and the Staff Manual respectively. Title pages will be prepared in manuscript.

WAR DIARY
or
~~INTELLIGENCE SUMMARY.~~
(Erase heading not required.)

1st Bn Leicestershire Regt.

Place	Date	Hour	Summary of Events and Information	Remarks and references to Appendices
TOURMIGNIES	15	0900-0930	Drill & P.T. remainder of morning Education & Salvage	1916
Start 14/9 1/10000	16		Church Parade as usual	1916
	17		Detachment sent on duty, no Railway Parade	1916
	18	0930	Drill P.T. Education & Salvage work carried out. Musketry carried out on Range by B Coy, remainder usual routine	1916
	19	0915-1015	Education 1030-1230 Musketry on Range	1916
	20	0900-1000	Drill P.T. 1000-1100 Education remainder of morning Musketry	1916
	21		Same Routine as previous day	1916
	22	0900-1000	Drill 1000-1100 Education 1115-1230 Education fire on Range. Battn Team playing M.G.C. at Association Football	1916
	23		Church Parade as usual	1916
	24	0900-1000	Drill & P.T. remainder of morning as usual	1916
	25		Same routine as for 24th	1916
	26		Same routine as y'day	1916
	27	0900-0730	Drill P.T. Battn employed in Rem: Street of pt Back football held Bombardier and won	1916
	28	0900-0730	Drill P.T. remainder of morning as usual	1916

E. B. Oliver Capt
OC 1/4 Leicestershire Regt

Army Form C. 2118.

ORDERLY ROOM
No. HE 1984
Date 2.4.19
14th Leicestershire Regt.

Secret

WAR DIARY
or
INTELLIGENCE SUMMARY
(Erase heading not required.)

4 APR 19

11 Leicesters

16 8

Place	Date	Hour	Summary of Events and Information	Remarks and references to Appendices
TOURMIGNIES Sept. 1918/Mar 1919	March 1919 1	0900-1030	Physical Training & Drill. Photo played in Event 2 "Photo Competition"	142D
	2		Entries completition first.	142D
			Church Parade as usual	142D
	3		March Routine 16732 Pte Chase W.E 54385 Pte Owens marched Military etc	142D
	4	0700-0930	Drill & P.T. Remained of morning Colonys etc	142D
	5		Usual Routine Special service for Ash Wednesday	142D
	6			140D
	7	0700-0930	Drill PT Games etc drainage Library etc	
	8		Brig RB Okey M.C. presented on leave	130D
	9		Church Parade as usual. St Eve Envoy reported lost from Lives	180D
	10	0700 to 0730 do PT + Drill arrived at Arges in usual carrying report etc kits ets	64
	11 12 15			
	16		Church Parade as usual. Royal Engineers band played at ATTICHES	144D
			from 1500hrs to 1600hrs	

Secret.   Army Form C. 2118.

WAR DIARY
or
INTELLIGENCE SUMMARY.

1st Leicesters

(Erase heading not required.)

Place	Date	Hour	Summary of Events and Information	Remarks and references to Appendices
TOURMIGNIES	March 1919			
	17		Usual drill. PT carried out. Arrangements being made at Templeuve	
Slept at ½/17 ½/ TOURM.	18		LO proceeded Templeuve on Traffic Guard duty at ST ANDRE	
	19		Passed as usual	
	20		2 Lieut O.W. Brumby left Batt. to join 2nd Bn Royal Berks Regt.	
	21		Horse Running	
	22		do	
	23		Church Parade as usual	
	24		Horses marched all day with draft in PETIT ATTICHES	
	25		Lieut J. LUTHY on TOUR MOVIES	
	26		2/Lt Angus + 9/ King arrived	
	27		Usual routine	
	28		" " Capt Ennis proceeded to take over Coy at St André	
	29		Usual routine	
	31		" Capt Otley left Unit for demobilization	

W. [signature]

Army Form C. 2118.

14th Bn Leicestershire Regt

WAR DIARY
or
INTELLIGENCE SUMMARY.
(Erase heading not required.)

Place	Date	Hour	Summary of Events and Information	Remarks and references to Appendices
	1		Usual Routine	
	2		Usual Routine	
	3	9:00	Usual Routine	
	4			
	5			
	6			
	7			
	8			
	9			
	10			
	11			
	12			
	13			
	14		Usual Routine	
	15		" "	
	16		Bn to ST ANDRÉ	

E.B. Clair Capt
COMMANDING 14th Bn. LEICESTERSHIRE REGT.

1 MAY 19

ORDERLY ROOM

No. 1/5/19

WAR DIARY 14th Bn. Leicestershire Regt. APRIL 1919

or

INTELLIGENCE SUMMARY

Army Form C. 2118.

(Erase heading not required.)

Place	Date	Hour	Summary of Events and Information	Remarks and references to Appendices

COMMANDING 14th Bn. LEICESTERSHIRE REGT.

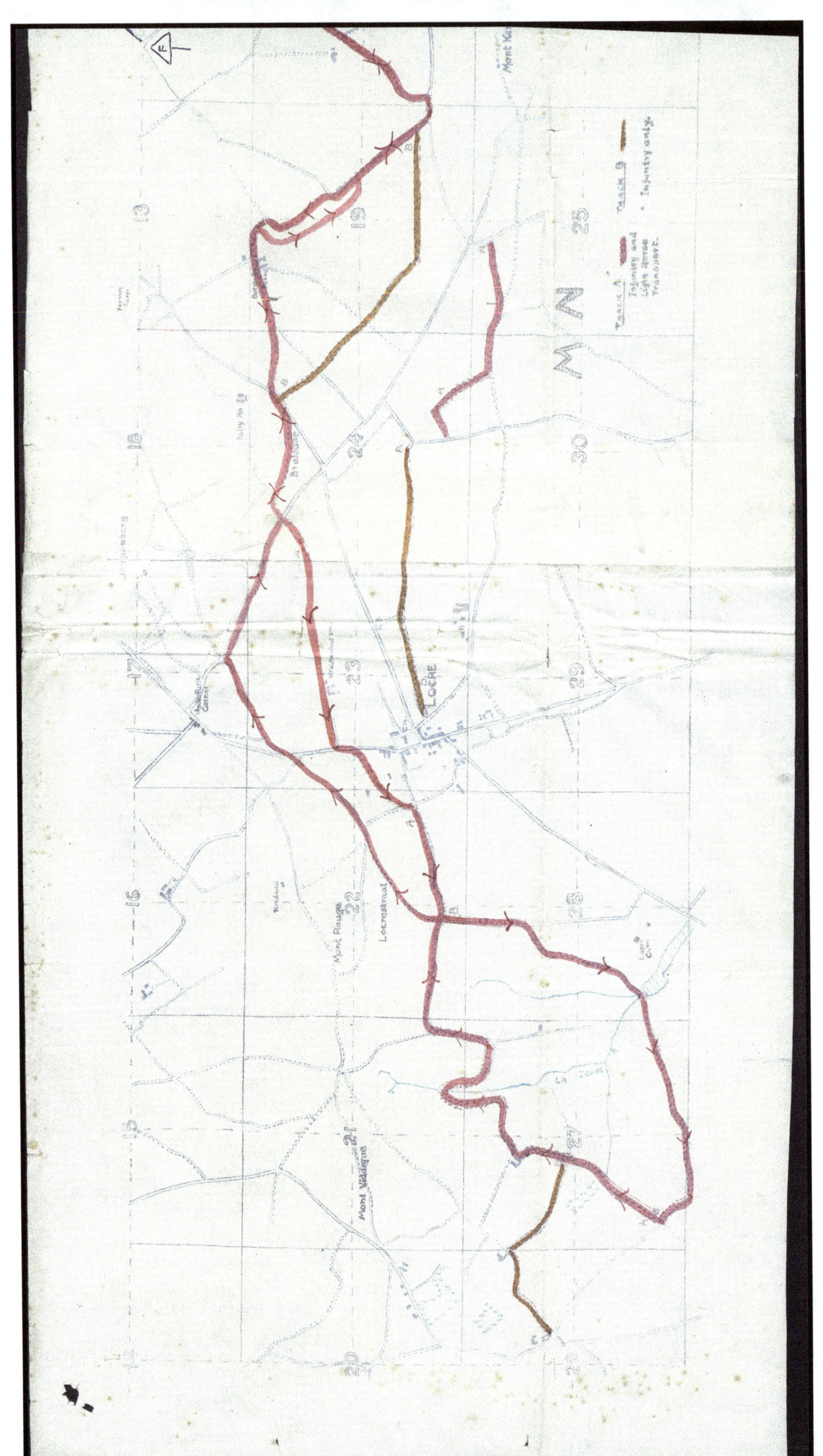

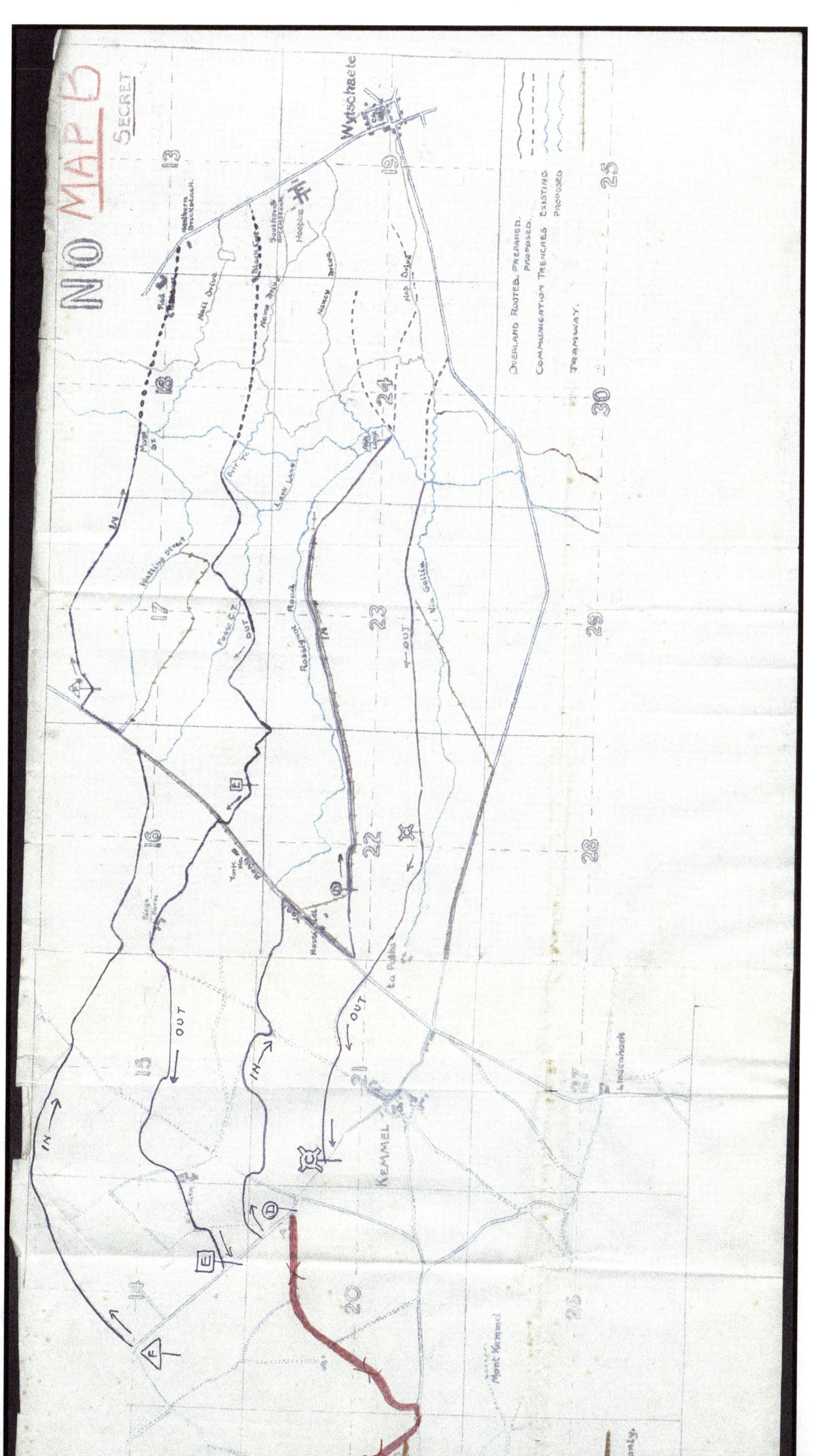

4.

Unit Commanders are reminded of the importance of sending to Brigade H.Q. frequent reports on the situation and the attitude of the enemy.

Brigade Headquarters will remain at THE RIB.

The 58th Inf. Bde. Forward Station will be at O.13.a.73.60.

47th Inf. Bde. Forward Station will be at N.24.b.6.0. After the BLACK LINE has been captured it will be at O.19.b.3.1.

12. CONTACT AEROPLANES

Contact Aeroplanes (Type R.E.8) will fly over the line and call for flares at the following hours :-

Zero plus 45 minutes.
Zero plus 2 hours.
Zero plus 4 hours 20 minutes.
Zero plus 5 hours 20 minutes.
Zero plus 6 hours 30 minutes.
Zero plus 11 hours.

Flares and Watson Fans should be shown only by the leading troops. Troops will be prepared to light flares at other times when called for by the aeroplanes.

13. SYNCHRONIZATION.

All units will send a watch to Brigade H.Q. at 9 a.m. 12 noon, 6 p.m. and 11 p.m. daily until Zero hour.

14. S.O.S. SIGNAL.

The S.O.S. Signal will remain as at present, - RED Signal Cartridges.

15. ZERO HOUR.

Zero hour will be notified later.

16. BRIGADE PRISONERS CAGE.

The Brigade Prisoners Cage where all prisoners will be sent, will be at Brigade H.Q. THE RIB.

17. INSTRUCTIONS.

Instructions for the attack have been issued from time to time in 49TH INFANTRY BRIGADE INSTRUCTIONS for the OFFENSIVE. These Instructions are hereby brought into force.

18. ACKNOWLEDGE.

J.W.B.D.Willcox Captain,
Brigade Major, 49th Infantry Brigade.

Issued through Signals at 1.50 P.M.

Copy No. 1 to G. O. C.
       2   2nd R. Irish Regt.
       3   7th R. Innis Fus.
       4   8th R. Innis Fus.
       5   7/8th R. Irish Fus.
       6   49th M.G.Compan
       7   49th T.M.Battery.
       8   16th Division
       9   47th Inf. Bde.
     10   48th Inf. Bde.
     11 to 58th Inf. Bde.
     12   57th Inf. Bde.
     13   Left Group.
     14   16th Div. Arty.
     15   157th Field Coy,R.E.
     16   11th Hants Pioneers.
     17   Bde. Intelligence Off.
     18-19 War Diary.
     20   File.

www.ingramcontent.com/pod-product-compliance
Lightning Source LLC
Chambersburg PA
CBHW081445160426
43193CB00013B/2393